Layman's Bible Book Commentary
Psalms

LAYMAN'S BIBLE BOOK COMMENTARY

L B B C

PSALMS

VOLUME 8

Alton H. McEachern

BROADMAN PRESS
Nashville, Tennessee

To
R. Betty Coleman McEachern
Companion of the Way

4211-78

ISBN: 0-8054-1178-X

Dewey Decimal Classification: 223.2

Subject heading: BIBLE O.T. PSALMS

Library of Congress Catalog Card Number: 79-56593

Printed in the United States of America

Foreword

The *Layman's Bible Book Commentary* in twenty-four volumes was planned as a practical exposition of the whole Bible for lay readers and students. It is based on the conviction that the Bible speaks to every generation of believers but needs occasional reinterpretation in the light of changing language and modern experience. Following the guidance of God's Spirit, the believer finds in it the authoritative word for faith and life.

To meet the needs of lay readers, the *Commentary* is written in a popular style, and each Bible book is clearly outlined to reveal its major emphases. Although the writers are competent scholars and reverent interpreters, they have avoided critical problems and the use of original languages except where they were essential for explaining the text. They recognize the variety of literary forms in the Bible, but they have not followed documentary trails or become preoccupied with literary concerns. Their primary purpose was to show what each Bible book meant for its time and what it says to our own generation.

The Revised Standard Version of the Bible is the basic text of the *Commentary*, but writers were free to use other translations to clarify an occasional passage or sharpen its effect. To provide as much interpretation as possible in such concise books, the Bible text was not printed along with the comment.

Of the twenty-four volumes of the *Commentary*, fourteen deal with Old Testament books and ten with those in the New Testament. The volumes range in pages from 140 to 168. Four major books in the Old Testament and five in the New are treated in one volume each. Others appear in various combinations. Although the allotted space varies, each Bible book is treated as a whole to reveal its basic message with some passages getting special attention. Whatever plan of Bible study the reader may follow, this *Commentary* will be a valuable companion.

Despite the best-seller reputation of the Bible, the average survey of Bible knowledge reveals a good deal of ignorance about it and its primary meaning. Many adult church members seem to think that its study is intended for children and preachers. But some of the newer translations have been making the Bible more readable for all ages. Bible study has branched out from Sunday into other days of the week, and into neighborhoods rather than just in churches. This *Commentary* wants to meet the growing need for insight into all that the Bible has to say about God and his world and about Christ and his fellowship.

BROADMAN PRESS

Contents

Introduction to the Psalms

The Psalter is the hymnbook of the ancient Israelites. It reflects their faith and has had great influence on Christian worship as well. The Psalms were collected over a period of many years. They were used in worship in the temple in Jerusalem and in the synagogues of later Judaism.

Some of the psalms are *general hymns of praise* suitable for use on any occasion. The *enthronement psalms* celebrate the Lord as King over the nation and the world. There are also *Songs of Zion* which focus on the Holy City, Jerusalem, and worship in its Temple.

Many of the psalms are *laments* of individuals asking deliverance from sickness or enemies. Other psalms are national laments sung in times of crisis and distress. We also find *hymns of trust* in which individuals express their faith in God and his willingness to bless. There are *thanksgivings*, as well, expressing gratitude for divine deliverance. Many of the psalms celebrate God's mighty acts on behalf of his people in the history of the nation, especially the Exodus.

There are *royal psalms* used at the coronation of a Davidic king or perhaps at royal weddings. The Psalms also contain *wisdom literature* which reflects on the meaning of life and the wisdom of God. A number of the psalms are written in *liturgical* form for use in public worship. A priest would recite certain verses, and the choir or congregation would make an antiphonal response or give a refrain.

Like the Pentateuch (the first five books of the Bible, the books of law), the Psalter is divided into five books.

The titles of the psalms are apparently the work of later editors who made the hymn collection. Often they contain musical directions such as: "To the choirmaster: with stringed instruments" (Pss. 4,6, etc.). The meaning of some of the technical Hebrew musical terms has been lost. Obviously, this does not affect the meaning or interpretation of the psalms themselves.

The Songs of Ascents (Pss. 120—134) are the hymns of pilgrims going up to Jerusalem to worship. Jerusalem is in the mountains, and one must "go up" to reach it from any direction.

Almost half the psalms are ascribed to David, the poet-king of Israel (2 Sam. 23:1). We do not know the meaning of the word *Selah* in some of the psalms. It may have been a call for a pause in the service.

The spiritual depth and beauty of the Psalms have made them a treasured resource for devotion, both public and private, for centuries. Their appeal has been virtually universal. They have played a prominent part in both Jewish and Christian worship for centuries.

Jesus' own devotional life was nourished on the Psalms. At his baptism the confirmation of his mission as Messiah included quotations from Psalm 2:7 and Isaiah 42:1 (see Luke 3:22). The song Jesus and his disciples sang at the Last Supper was probably the Hallel (Pss. 115—118). In agony on the cross Jesus recited Psalm 22:1, "My God, my God, why hast thou forsaken me?" (Matt. 27:46). His dying words were from Psalm 31:5, according to Luke 23:46: "And when Jesus had cried with a loud voice, he said, Father, into thy hands I commend my spirit: and having said thus, he gave up the ghost" (KJV).

The early Christian church took the pattern for much of its worship from the synagogue. This included singing the Psalms. (See such passages as Acts 16:25; Eph. 5:19; Col. 3:16.) The Psalms and the prophecy of Isaiah are the Old Testament books most often quoted in the New Testament.

The language of the Psalms is simple. A child can understand the meaning of many of the psalms. Yet the thought and theology of the Psalms is often profound. The Psalms express many varied human moods: praise and lament, repentance and joy, cursing and blessing, doubt and strong faith, love and hatred, fear and faith. The psalmists wrestle with the great issues of life: the problems of suffering, sin, and death. Rhodes calls the Psalms "the faith of the Old Testament set to music."[1]

It is difficult to date many of the psalms. They were written over a period of many years, from the beginning of the nation of Israel (around the time of King David, 1000 BC) until well after the Babylonian Exile (587-538 BC). Some of the psalms may be as late as 300 BC. The word *psalm* in Hebrew simply means "praises."

The Psalms reflect the theology of Israel much as our hymns and gospel songs show what Christians believe. Note some themes in the Psalms.

God's activity is an important theme in the Psalms. He is the *Creator* who spoke the world into existence and made humanity. He also sustains both by his power (see Ps. 33). God made Israel a nation—and made other nations, as well (Pss. 100:3; 86:9).

God also *saves* his people. Salvation is a general concept which includes deliverance from suffering, death, and sin. Salvation was viewed in the Psalms as being both material and spiritual.

The psalmists genuinely hated their enemies and vividly cursed them. Christians know that Jesus taught us to love our enemies (Matt. 5:44). The Hebrews lived by another principle, "Eye for eye, tooth for tooth" (Ex. 21:24). The cursing psalms reflect this view and remind us of the poets' humanity—and our own. The psalms show no full doctrine of life after death. Sheol was believed to be the abode of both the wicked and the righteous dead.

God is *sovereign*; he reigns in power in the Psalms. He is not to be compared with pagan deities or idols. As King, God is also the Judge of humanity. He both redeems and condemns, but redemption is his primary purpose (Ps. 72:1-4). God is concerned with both justice and mercy.

God *chose* Israel as his people and made a covenant with them. God's election of them included privilege, but it also required their obedience and service.

God *reveals* himself and his purpose by word and deed (33:4-7). He discloses himself in nature, law, and Israel's history and worship.

The nature of God is beautifully revealed in the theology of the Psalms. God is *holy*. He is other than mankind—far above us, yet never far from us. He is righteous.

God is also characterized by his *faithful love* (25:6-7; 103:4, 10-12). His grace is always more than we deserve. He can be depended on. God is true to his covenant promises even when people are not.

God is *spirit*; his power is at work in both the world and human history. The Psalms are also consistent with the rest of the Old Testament, insisting that God is *one*. Monotheism is clearly taught in the Psalms.

Erik Routley contends that the Psalms are a mirror of life.[2] They

reflect more than the life of ancient Israel. The Psalms give us meaningful insights into human nature—which is the same in modern
times as in ancient ones. The Psalms call us to worship and direct our
attention to the One who is worthy of our adoration. In our private
devotion, as well as public worship, the Psalms as a whole, not
simply the favorite ones, are a rich resource. The book begins with
the beatitude "Blessed is the man" and closes with the command
"Praise the Lord!" The overall theme of the Psalms is the presence of
God and our worship of him. They are an account of the encounter
of God and people—and they contribute to that continuing encounter.

Notes

1. Arnold B. Rhodes, *Layman's Bible Commentary* (Richmond: John
Knox Press, 1960), vol. 9, p. 8.
2. Erik Routley, *Exploring the Psalms* (Philadelphia: Westminster Press,
1975), p. 11.

Psalm 1: In Search of Happiness

Psalm 1 is the prologue to the entire Psalter. It is a preface poem to introduce the hymnbook of the Hebrew faith. The author presented two groups of persons often depicted in the Psalms—the righteous and the wicked. The righteous are friends of God who live in obedience to the covenant. The wicked are enemies of God who are rebellious against his will.

The Psalm accurately reflects classic Old Testament theology: the righteous prosper and the wicked perish. There are exceptions to this, such as Job. The basic premise of the psalm is the psalm is the happiness of the righteous and the ruin of the wicked.

A parallel to this passage is found in Jeremiah 17:5-8. In that poem the author contended, "Cursed is the man who trusts in man . . . " and "Blessed is the man who trusts in the Lord." Jeremiah contrasted the wicked (a worthless shrub in the desert) with the righteous (a tree planted by the water).

Happy Is the Righteous Man (1:1-3)

The psalm begins with a beatitude—an invocation of blessing and congratulations. It could be translated, "O how happy is the person who . . .!"

Some negatives are found in the Psalms. We are accustomed to positives. But we must first learn to say no to evil and wrong. Only then can we say yes to good. Each time a decision is made we set a priority. This involves saying both yes and no.

In broad strokes the psalmist powerfully presented the negatives in verse 1. The righteous man:

"Walks not in the counsel of the wicked." He does not take the advice of evil men for his guide.

"Nor stands in the way of sinners." He does not loiter with those who are habitual moral failures.

"Nor sits in the seat of scoffers." He does not become one who scorns the sacred and mocks God.

Notice the progression here, "walks, stands, sits." Evil grows. Sin may begin quite simply, but it becomes more serious.

On the positive side, the righteous person finds his delight in the law of the Lord (v. 2). His joy is to meditate on the teachings of Scripture and the revealed will of God. He marches to the sound of a different drum, following God's guidance rather than the world's shallow wisdom. The term *law* (Torah) is broader than the Ten Commandments or the first five books of the Bible. It includes all the revelation of God to humanity. Meditation involves taking the Word seriously by our determining to make use of more than a casual and occasional reading of the Bible. This verse is a deliberate contrast to verse 1.

The righteous person is like a tree carefully planted beside streams of water (v. 3). The implication here is that the tree has been lovingly transplanted by the Gardener where it can grow best. Spiritual happiness is not a right or natural circumstance. Happiness is God-given, not a human achievement.

It is important that the tree be planted where there is an ample water supply. In the dry country of Palestine rain does not fall four months in the year; if the winter rains fail to come, disaster threatens all growing things. Those who live there say, "Where there is water there is life. Where there is no water there is no life."

Note that the tree tended by the heavenly Gardener is fruitful in its season. This means both joy and usefulness—fulfilling its purpose.

Its leaf does not wither. The evergreen is symbolic of immortality. The tree flourishes. In all he does, the righteous person prospers and is blessed. He is "planted," sturdy, and able to survive the storms.

The righteous person of Psalm 1 is not perfect. He may not always be free of doubt, anxiety, or even the failure which is sin. But he is a growing, useful person, with purpose in living. His nourishment comes from God and his Word.

In verse 1 we are told what the righteous person does not do. In verse 2 we see what he does. In verse 3 we learn what he is like: a tree planted beside streams of water.

Disastrous Is the Fate of the Wicked (1:4-5)

Verse 4 begins emphatically, "The wicked are not so." *The New English Bible* translates the verse: "Wicked men are not like this; they are like chaff driven by the wind."

They are like worthless chaff blown away by the wind. Note the contrast with the stability of the tree planted by streams of water. Wheat was threshed by beating it on a hard surface to dislodge the grain. It was then tossed into the air. The heavy grain would fall back to the ground. But the light chaff or husks would be blown away by the wind. They were considered worthless. The wicked are just as unstable.

Verse 5 declares that the wicked cannot withstand the scrutiny of judgment. They have built on sand and will not endure once the time of testing comes. Their judgment may be both here and hereafter. The chaff is a symbol of rootlessness, fruitlessness, and objects having no value or future.

Conclusion (1:6)

In this final verse the psalmist set out two "ways" and contrasted them. The "way" is the life-style or orientation of a person.

The way of the righteous.—God knows and has a relationship with the righteous person. This person has divine approval, not because his is perfect but because he loves God and is growing in his likeness. This road leads to God.

The way of the wicked.—This way is a dead end. It leads no place except to destruction. Wicked persons exemplify the blowing chaff rather than a rooted tree. The wicked shall perish. Recall the twelve-year leadership of Hitler in Nazi Germany and its end product, disaster.

Only Christ is the perfectly righteous man, completely fulfilling the Father's will. His cross will result in our access to the tree of life within paradise. (See Rev. 22:2.)

Psalm 1 calls for our responsible obedience to God. It sets in bold relief what matters most: faith and obedience. And it warns the faithless that their life-style leads to failure and destruction.

Psalm 2: The Laughter of God

In verse 4 the Almighty is depicted sitting in heaven laughing at the folly of rebellious people. It is a scene in which Puck's remark would fit. In Shakespeare's *A Midsummer Night's Dream* (III, ii.) Puck exclaims, "Lord, what fools these mortals be!" God must be amused at times by some of our antics.

Psalm 2 is a royal psalm, composed for the coronation of Israel's kings. It may have been recited by the king himself and appears to be based on Nathan's oracle in 2 Samuel 7:8-16. There significant promises were made to King David:

1. He is to rank among the world's greatest kings.
2. His kingdom will enjoy peace and freedom from aggression.
3. The dynasty he founds will endure forever.

4. God will be a Father to him and remember his covenant love
   toward him.

Later, Christians would apply this psalm to the ideal King, the Messiah, who is the Son of David.

Plotting Against the New King (2:1-3)

When a new king came to the throne, vassal nations under Israel's rule would plot revolt. This afforded an ideal time for them to break away. The psalmist was mystified at their futile conspiracy (v. 1). He saw their rebellion as being against the Lord, as well as against his "anointed" (literally "messiah"). Davidic kings were given the title "anointed." After the end of the monarchy in 586 BC, the term was used to refer to the ideal future king or Messiah. Peter quoted this passage in his sermon at Pentecost (see Acts 4:25-29).

God's Promises to the New King (2:4-9)

God is amused at the futility of the rebels. After all, it was he who had installed the king on "Zion, my holy hill."

Verse 7 contains an important messianic reference. It was quoted in Acts 13:33. The king became God's son. This was especially true of the Messiah: "You are my son, today I have begotten you." This truth was reflected in the baptism of Jesus (Luke 3:21) and is at the heart of the gospel: John 3:16.

The kings of Israel were considered God's adopted sons. Indeed, Israel itself was his adopted son (Hos. 11:1). By faith in Christ, believers are the adopted sons of God as well (Rom. 8:15). Jesus was God's unique Son, his "only begotten" (John 3:18; 20:31; Rom. 1:4).

Those who rebel against the Lord's "anointed" encounter the Lord's severe judgment (v. 9). Note this sequence in the psalm. God's messianic Son is described in terms of

1. His relationship with the Lord—he is his begotten Son (v. 7).
2. His heritage—the nations of the earth (v. 8).
3. His might and power—with an iron scepter, he breaks them like so much pottery.

Exhortation to Submit (2:10-11)

The psalmist (and the new king) sounded a warning to those who are rebellious (v. 10). The rebels were admonished to serve the Lord reverently and respectfully—lest they perish (v. 11)

A Beatitude (2:12)

Those who find their security in the Lord and his king are to be congratulated. They will be happy indeed.

These royal psalms nourished the messianic hope for centuries after the end of the historic Davidic monarchy. Israel still believed God's promises to David would one day be fulfilled. Indeed, they were. In the person and ministry of Jesus, the kingdom of God was inaugurated on earth. He will one day shatter the forces of evil (Rev. 12:5; 19:15).

Psalm 3: God Is Our Shield

This is the first in a series of psalms attributed to King David (Ps. 3—41). They were either written by him or later Davidic kings. The setting given in the title of this psalm is David's flight before the army of Absalom, his rebellious son (2 Sam. 15—19). The psalm was probably used by both David and his successors. It is also appropriate for use by the individual worshiper who is in distress. The theme of the Psalm is faith in God, who hears our prayers and protects us from evil.

The World's Taunts (3:1-2)

The psalmist poured out his heart to God in distress over his enemies. His foes might have been other nations, rebels within his own realm, or, more generally, the forces of evil. Two things are pointed out: they are against us, and they mock our faith and reliance on God (v. 2).

The Believer's Unwavering Trust in God (3:3-6)

1. *God is our shield* against evil, our protection in trouble. He protects us, whether from literal arrows or slanderous words. God's glory is his radiant presence. To speak of glory is to say God is with his own, lifting them up (v. 3). *Sursum Corda* is an ancient word of encouragement used in worship. It means "Lift up your heart!" God *lifts* up our heads. When we are dejected and depressed, we look down. God encourages us, enabling us to stand erect and "walk tall." Recall the portrait of brooding President Kennedy, which is on display at the White House.

2. *God answers prayer* (v. 4). The psalmist prayed confidently, "He answers me." This confidence in prayer is seen in Jesus' petition at Lazarus' tomb (John 11:41-43). "His holy hill" is Mount Zion. There the Temple was built. It represented God's presence on earth.

3. *God sustains us* as we go about our daily routine (v. 5). The psalmist could sleep with confidence in God's protection. He was at peace.

Sleep is a great curative, "that knits up the ravell'd sleave of care" (Shakespeare, *Macbeth*, II, ii). Recall that God's cure for Elijah's discouragement was food, rest, and reassurance (1 Kings 19).

4. *We need not live in fear* (v. 6). Though our enemies are many, whether nations or a mob, we can have confident faith in God.

The Believer's Confident Assurance (3:7-8)

"Arise, O Lord!" is thought to be the ancient battle cry of Israel's army. Here the psalmist pleaded for deliverance. The word used literally means "salvation." He would be saved from his enemies by the Lord. God would "smite" them on the cheek (an insulting gesture) and "break the teeth of the wicked" (render them powerless). He would pull the tiger's teeth! Thus, the psalmist had complete confidence in God's victory.

Selah

This is the first psalm in which this word occurs. It is found seventy-one times in the psalms. Scholars are not certain what it means. Apparently, it was a word of instruction to the musicians when the psalm was used in Temple worship. It may have called for an instrumental interlude. (See the *Broadman Bible Commentary*, Vol. 4, p. 175, for a discussion of its possible meanings.) The word *Selah*, like the titles on the psalms, is a marginal notation, believed to have been added by editors long after the original hymns were composed.

Psalm 4: The Happy Heart

This psalm begins with a plea for help (v. 1), but turns out to be a strong affirmation of personal faith. Sincere faith in God is a source of comfort and peace, whatever outward circumstances may be.

This is the first of fifty-five psalms with instructions to the choirmaster in its title, "with stringed instruments." This probably called for a quiet musical background for the reading or singing of the psalm in public worship. The stringed instruments would likely include the lyre and harp (Pss. 150:3; 49:4).

A Plea to God (4:1)

The psalmist was in trouble, but he did not despair. He felt confident, based on past experience in which God has answered his prayers. "O

God of my right!" is a Hebrew idiom. The psalmist meant he could depend on God to vindicate him—heaven would uphold the rightness of his cause. Past experiences of grace gave him confidence in the present. Thus, faith grows.

Counsel for People (4:2-6)

The enemies of the psalmist had held him up to ridicule. He accused them of loving empty words and lies (v. 2). They were persons who were indifferent to God. They had no time for spiritual matters and made sport of his faith. They busied themselves chasing delusions (material things which, though important, do not satisfy soul hunger).

Those who are godly belong to the Lord, and he hears their prayers (v. 3). The psalmist received God's steadfast love, and he was committed to the Lord in loving steadfastness. Faith and faithfulness were his grateful responses to grace.

The psalmist could withstand his enemies' ridicule. Next, he offered them some advice (vv. 4-5).

"Be angry, but sin not," he counseled. The apostle Paul quoted this verse in his practical exhortation in Ephesians 4:26, going on to say, "Do not let the sun go down on your anger." Nursed anger is self-destructive.

The psalmist advised them to meditate on the things of God as they lay quietly in bed. Apparently, the persons the psalmist was addressing had expected a lot from their religion—without putting much into it. They had "tipped" the Lord, but then expected him to bless them with great prosperity. He advised them to "offer right sacrifices." That is, their worship was to come from grateful hearts and be matched with ethical living. Then they could put their "trust in the Lord" (v. 5). This kind of worship would show that they stand in a right relationship with the Lord.

The persons being addressed appeared to be troubled by doubts (v. 6). They said, "O that we might see some good!" They expected prosperity and success. Why didn't they enjoy good crops and fruitful herds? The second half of the verse contains their prayer for the Lord to look on them with favor. Theirs was a practical religion, a success cult. That type of faith has it rough when things aren't going well. A Pollyanna religion does very well as long as the sun shines. But when the dark of suffering and trouble comes, it is not substantial. "Why doesn't the Lord bless us?" they asked.

The Joy of a Happy Heart (4:7-8)

By contrast, the psalmist could sing about joy and peace even in the time of adversity. He had greater "joy" in his heart than those who delighted in bumper crops of grain and grapes (v. 7). This inner gladness comes from a right relationship with God. It is not controlled by external circumstances. If our happiness is tied to prosperity and things, it may go up and down like a thermometer. When it depends on our daily walk with the Lord, it can be much more constant. The poet's joy came from God alone. (Compare such passages as Matt. 6:33 and Phil. 4:11.)

The psalmist not only had joy in the Lord; he also experienced "peace" (v. 8). He could go to bed and sleep because of his perfect trust in the Lord. Anxiety is the lot of us all at times. Faithful trust is an important part of its cure. The problems we face have solutions. We are to work toward those solutions, whether they are medical or circumstantial. Other troubles are part of life which we cannot control. We are to accept these, asking the Father's grace to make us adequate. Even in the dark valleys of suffering we can have an inner peace because God is with us. He alone enables us to "dwell in safety."

For those who are in Christ, not even death itself need hold any ultimate dread. The psalmist affirmed that he could sleep without fear. Such peace and joy is reflected in the promise of Jesus to his disciples: "You have sorrow now, but I will see you again and your hearts will rejoice, and no one will take your joy from you" (John 16:22).

The radiant faith in God depicted in this psalm prefigures Christ. Recall such scenes from the Gospels as: Christ asleep during the storm at sea (Matt. 8:24); Christ telling his disciples to "Seek first his kingdom and his righteousness, and all these things shall be yours as well" (Matt. 6:33); his constant faith in the Father's will even in the garden of Gethsemane (Matt. 26:39). Jesus was like the man of faith and inner joy described in the psalm.

Psalm 5: Words and Signs

This psalm is a morning prayer. It would have been sung in the Temple at dawn as the morning sacrifice was offered. While it is a plea for deliverance from enemies, it is even more an affirmation of the worshiper's faith.

The psalmist affirmed his confidence that:

1. God will hear and answer his prayer.

2. God opposes and hates evil.

3. God is gracious in his protection of his own—he is their shield.

Note in the title the request for the psalm to be accompanied by the playing of flutes. Imagine the scene in which this psalm was sung: The sun rises over the Mount of Olives and reflects off the bronze doors of the Temple into the courtyard filled with worshipers. The effect is almost that of a double sunrise! Smoke climbs upward from the altar as the morning sacrifice is consumed. Priests scurry busily about their duties. Then worshipers grow quiet at the sound of flutes. They are melodic and Oriental. The temple choir sings the psalm antiphonally—half sing verses 1-3, and then the others sing verses 4-6, etc. The congregation waits before the Lord in anticipation.

The Morning Petition (5:1-3)

Of the appointed times for worship at the Temple, the morning seems to be the most important. There are numerous references to morning prayer in the Psalms (88:13).

Three times the psalmist prayed, "Give ear . . . heed . . . hearken." This was to emphasize the urgency of his request. He addressed the Almighty as "my King and my God." This could mean the psalm was sung by the king of Israel, recognizing God as his King. More likely, it is simply the worshiper's recognition of divine might—defeating evil and upholding good.

In verse 1 he spoke of "my words" and "my groanings." The latter word may refer to his stammering or halting prayer. It is translated, "Consider my inmost thoughts" (NEB). He was confident, expecting an answer to his prayer (v. 3).

God Hates Evil (5:4-6)

The psalmist told God about his enemies. They were boastful, liars, bloodthirsty, and deceitful—not a complimentary report. They were the enemies of both God and his people.

The psalmist said that God "hatest all evildoers" (v. 5). That may not be the way Christians would state it. We would say that God hates sin but loves the sinner. But don't forget: judgment is the underside of God's love. Those who spurn his love incur his wrath. Note Jesus' comments in Matthew 23:13-36.

Worship in God's House (5:7-8)

The psalmist did not claim to be sinless but he did trust in God's

steadfast love. He was in covenant relationship with his Maker and worshiped facing the holy of holies, which represents God's presence on
Earth (v. 7).

He prayed for divine leadership. This was his principal petition. His
enemies lay in wait for him. (The word here translated *enemies* means
those who lurk.) They would lead him astray. Therefore, he prayed that
God would lead him in a straight way.

His Enemies' Deceit (5:9-10)

This passage is similar to verses 4-6. His enemies were totally untrust-
worthy. Their words were as dangerous as an unmarked open tomb.
Whoever said, "Words can't hurt me"? These verses sound like a description of modern political terrorists.

God Shields His Own (5:11-12)

Those who trust in the Lord may rejoice in his protection. He defends
them, and they are safe. God's grace is the shield of the faithful, protecting them from harm. The emphasis on the grace of God is strong in this
psalm. Because of grace, the psalmist expected God to answer his
prayers, guide him in the right way, and protect him from vengeful
enemies.

Psalm 6: A Prayer for Healing

The title calls for the singing of this psalm to be accompanied with
stringed instruments. This is the first of the "seven penitential psalms"
often used in Christian worship (see also Pss. 32; 38; 51; 102; 130; 143).

Remember that in Old Testament times suffering was thought to be
caused by sin. Often we suffer due to sin, but not always. There is also
the suffering of the innocent. This was the theme of the book of Job (see
John 9:1-3).

A Prayer for Healing (6:1-5)

The psalmist was sick in both body and soul. "My bones" represent his
very being. The whole person was ill. He pleaded, "How long?" The sick
wonder if they will ever be well again. He prayed for divine healing,
looking to the trustworthy love of God (v. 4).

"Sheol" was the name used for the abode of the dead in the Old Testament. It was seen as a silent underworld in which the dead were "shades" who had a shadowy existence but no real life. The psalmist contended that if he died, he could not praise God in death. Christians believe in life after because of Jesus' resurrection. He conquered death and Sheol, giving us the hope of Paradise.

Grief Described (6:6-7)

The psalmist described his suffering in terms of weariness, weeping, and weakness. The taunts of his foes made the ordeal harder still to bear. Tears and moans were his lot.

Answered Prayer (6:8-10)

The tone of the psalm changes abruptly. The psalmist experienced healing. Like Job's comforters, his enemies troubled him. Now he was vindicated before them. God heard and answered his prayer, delivering him from sickness unto death.

Guilt is often part of our grief when illness comes. We ask questions like, "Why has this happened to me?" It helps to remember that not all suffering is due to our sins.

Psalm 7: God, the Righteous Judge

The psalmist lamented his enemies' accusations and declared his oath of innocence.

Cry for Deliverance (7:1-2)

The writer stated his faith in God and pleaded for deliverance. In the Psalms, salvation most often means deliverance from peril. That basic concept was later expanded to include spiritual salvation from the power of evil. The psalmist's enemies were like a dangerous lion that would destroy him (v. 2).

Declaration of Innocence (7:3-5)

Having been accused of dishonesty, the writer called on God to curse him if he were guilty. Here he was not claiming moral perfection. He simply insisted on his innocence concerning his enemies' accusations. If he were guilty of wrong, he prayed that God would let his enemies: 1. overtake him; 2. trample him; and 3. lay him in the dust.

God, the Righteous Judge (7:6-11)

The psalmist asked that God hold court and establish his integrity. He knew justice was on his side because he was not guilty. The poet had every confidence that he would be vindicated by God, the righteous judge (v. 11).

The Boomerang of Evil (7:12-16)

Those who refuse to repent incur God's wrath and judgment. God was depicted as using a soldier's weapons: a sharp sword, powerful bow, and fiery arrows (vv. 12-13).

The metaphor used in verse 14 is vivid: the evil person conceives evil, is pregnant with mischief, and gives birth to lies (see Jas. 1:13-15).

Evil attitudes and actions backfire on us. An evil person digs a trap for someone else and falls into it himself (v. 15). Evil done to others comes back on our own heads (v. 15). What we reap we sow; the measure we give is the measure we get back, whether good or bad (see Matt. 7:1-2). He who hates another hurts himself. This law of the spiritual life is reflected in the psalm.

A Vow (7:17)

The final verse is a sacred promise of praise. The writer declared that he would not fail to be grateful for his deliverance. Anyone would pray in a pinch. But not everyone would remember to be grateful after the trouble passed. Recall the story of ten lepers who were healed by the Master—only one returned to give thanks.

Psalm 8: What Is Man?

This psalm begins and ends with adoration of God. David was moved to praise by the starry heavens above and the dignity of man. The poem is the creation story set to music. It is both simple and beautiful.

Even little children join in praise of the Creator (v. 2). Jesus quoted this verse in Matthew 21:16. God chooses the weak things to amaze the mighty (1 Cor. 1:27). He is full of surprises! Who would have expected him to come to earth in such a humble setting as Bethlehem?

God's Glory in Creation (8:3-4)

God as Creator is a major theme in the Psalms. Note the fine poetic touch, "thy heavens, the work of thy fingers"—some needlework!

In light of the vast expansiveness of space, man appears insignificant (v. 4). When we consider all of creation, man is but a speck of cosmic dust—but he is a thinking speck, made in the image of his Creator!

What Is Man? (8:4)

This is the haunting question of the ages. It has been asked by every philosopher and theologian, as well as every thinking person. The paradox is apparent. Compared to the universe, man is puny and insignificant. Yet, since he is made in the image of God, man has great worth and potential for fellowship with his Maker.

What is man? Darwin might see him as a monkey's orphan, the end product of evolution. Marx might view man as an economic tool. Freud thought man a bundle of sexual drives. But man is more than a monkey or money or a sex maniac. These are all incomplete views of man.

The Bible views mankind as having a dual nature—"kin to God and kin to the clod." He has been called the great amphibian: made for two worlds. Man is a creature made from the dust of the earth. Yet he is more than a clothed ape. Man is made in the image of his Creator. He has the capacity for the spiritual fellowship of a potential child of God. Man is both an earthling and a being made for the heavens. David was aware of both man's insignificance and his importance.

Man, the Crown of Creation (8:5-8)

"The son of man" (mere, mortal man) is made in the likeness of God. This title was used in the New Testament of Jesus as representative of humanity. Man is crowned (encircled) with glory and honor and given dominion over creation (Gen. 1:26 f.). Man has harnessed both wild horses and atoms, fulfilling the divine command.

Although no one knows what the setting of Psalm 8 was, two possibilities are Solomon's Temple or the awe-inspiring sight of the sky at night, built by God himself.

Jesus fulfilled the perfect image of God in man. (See Col. 1:15 and Gal. 2:20.)

Psalm 9: Protector of the Poor

Psalms 9 and 10 were originally one psalm and are so translated in ancient Greek and Latin Bibles. They have a common alphabetical framework. An acrostic is used with lines of the two psalms beginning with the letters of the Hebrew alphabet. Psalm 9 is a hymn of praise, and Psalm 10 is a lament.

A Call to Thanksgiving (9:1-4)

The wonderful acts of God are a cause for praise and thanksgiving. These include his mighty acts on behalf of his people Isarel (vv. 1-2). The psalmist has personally found God acting on his behalf, as well (vv. 3-4).

A Hymn of Praise (9:5-14)

God is the righteous Judge of both mankind and nations. His judgment is final. Note the strong verbs in verses 5 and 6: "rebuked, destroyed, blotted out." The "very memory" of God's enemies will fade and perish.

God is securely enthroned and judges "with equity" (vv. 7-8). He is the believer's stronghold (vv. 9-10). The divine faithfulness calls forth praise (vv. 11-12).

A personal petition, like that in verses 1-4, is sounded again (vv. 13-14). The psalmist was spared at "the gates of death." Old Testament men had no clear hope of life after death. Therefore, the prospect of death must have been more fearful for them than later for Christians. The gates of death cannot withstand the risen Christ and his victorious church (Matt. 16:18).

Judgment on the Nations (9:15-20)

Nations which forget God find themselves ensnared in their own evil devices (vv. 15-16). They go down to the abode of the dead, Sheol (v. 17). Divine judgment is not limited to some far-off future event. It occurs here and now as well. The final verse in this psalm is a potent prayer, "Let the nations know that they are but men!"—a timely reminder. (See Isa. 40:15.)

God is the champion of the poor and needy. They will not be overlooked or allowed to perish (v. 18). They can depend on God.

Psalm 10: The Way the Wicked Think

The Absence of God (10:1-2)

The psalmist was troubled by the apparent absence of God. He seemed to be in hiding, allowing the wicked to enjoy a field day. The silence of God is often a problem for believers. This may be God's way of teaching his children to walk by faith.

The truth of Christmas and the incarnation is that "the hidden God" has revealed himself in his Son. He is among us, and he is for us. His name is Emmanuel!

The Boasts of the Wicked (10:3-13)

God's apparent absence made the wicked bold. In this psalm, they were not atheists but secular Jews. They contended:

1. "There is no God" (v. 4). This is the apex of human pride.

2. "I shall not meet adversity" (v. 6). Therefore, they proceeded to prey on the poor, fearing no punishment.

3. "God has forgotten . . . he will never see" (v. 11). Even if there is a God, it makes no difference, they thought. He does not care. But a God who does not care does not count. He does not withhold his anger forever!

4. God will never "call to account." They felt sure of this (v. 13). Therefore, they thought they were immune from divine judgment. Human arrogance knows no limits.

But God Does See (10:14-18)

God is aware. He is neither asleep nor uncaring. The helpless ("fatherless") trust in him and will not be disappointed (v. 14). In due course God will punish the evildoer (v. 15). Never forget that "the Lord is king for ever" while nations rise and fall. He is the one constant in the midst of change.

God will hear the prayer of the meek and deliver the oppressed (vv. 17-18). They will not always have to live in terror.

How different are the judgments of God! He looks on the intention of the heart and judges fairly. He does not run his world on our timetable. But never forget, he is King and is in ultimate control of history.

Psalm 11: "Flee Like a Bird"

This psalm is a gem of trust in God. The psalmist was in danger. He was advised to "flee like a bird to the mountains" (v. 1). But he would not take refuge in the hill country. Though his cause appeared hopeless, he affirmed his faith in God. Trust is the theme here.

Faith Over Fear (11:1-3)

God is our refuge. This truth is characteristic of many of the psalms (see 7; 16; 31; 57; 71). The psalmist's faith was even more vivid when seen against the backdrop of his friends' fear. Moral foundations were crumbling (v. 3). The psalmist was fighting for a lost cause, in a hopeless situation. Still, he affirmed his unshaken faith in God.

But God (11:4-7)

God is in his holy temple on earth, and on his throne in heaven—he sees and knows. God is still with his people, and he is still in control (v. 4). The following excerpt from James Russell Lowell's poem "The Present Crisis" speaks of God's care and watchfulness for his children:

> Careless seems the great Avenger; history's pages but record
> One death-grapple in the darkness 'twixt old systems and the
> Word;
> Truth forever on the scaffold, Wrong forever on the throne,—
> Yet that scaffold sways the future, and, behind the dim
> unknown,
> Standeth God within the shadow, keeping watch above his own.

The psalmist's friends looked at outward circumstances and felt despair. He looked in faith toward God and was optimistic.

God will test and prove both the righteous (person of faith) and the wicked (faithless). His test will be like the refiner's fire which separates gold from base metals. His judgment will be harsh. The upright will survive it, while the faithless are destroyed. The psalmist's confidence in God was unshaken; he was a man of courage.

The psalmist's was a realistic faith. Despite troubled times he knew he was not alone or without divine help. He refused to save his own skin. He sought not escape, but the Lord.

This is a psalm of confident faith.

Psalm 12: God's Pure Promises

The psalmist lived in a time of moral bankruptcy. Persons of integrity were rare (as they always are). People were trusting in themselves and living as practical atheists. Feeling as Elijah did, that there were no righteous persons left, he called out to the Lord for help. (See 1 Kings 19:10,14.)

A Cry For Help (12:1-4)

Godly people were few and far between, if not extinct (v. 1). This is poetic overstatement to make a point. Men in positions of leadership were liars and guilty of flattery. Someone has said that flattery is like perfume: OK if you sniff it, dangerous if you swallow it.

These braggarts were deliberately deceiving others (v. 2). They spoke with mixed motives—a double heart. They had a hidden agenda. They followed an evil purpose (v. 4). It was a time of social corruption when men could not be trusted. They had perverted the gift of speech for selfish ends.

God's Bright Promises (12:5-6)

God promised to come to the aid of the poor and needy who were being oppressed (v. 5). The promises of God are as pure and precious as silver refined seven times (the number for perfection). The psalmist is here contrasting the trustworthy word of God with the flattery and lies of people. Human deceit is set over against God's dependability. His most perfect Word was made flesh in Jesus Christ.

The Renewed Appeal (12:7-8)

The poet turned from his consideration of the purity and beauty of the divine promises to his current situation. He asked again for protection from the wicked who appeared to have free rein. Human baseness was held high.

We can depend on the Word of God and his sure promises.

Psalm 13: Dark and Dawn

The setting of this psalm may be a time of sickness or the threat of a taunting enemy. It uses a common biblical theme: darkness and light, tragedy and triumph. (Note this theme in the Gospel of John.)

"How Long, O Lord?" (13:1-2)

The psalmist's strong lament was repeated four times for emphasis. He felt forgotten by God. (Every believer has such moments in crisis.) He felt abandoned. Was the Almighty playing hide and seek with him? He felt pain in his soul and had a sorrowful heart (v. 2). His enemies were in triumph.

The psalmist may sound harsh in his complaint. But notice that he was being honest with God. He was not guilty of any false piety, used to cover his true feelings. God respects the prayers of honest souls and answers those of desperate ones.

A Plea for God to Answer (13:3-4)

The poet pleaded for God to answer him. Otherwise, he might "sleep the sleep of death" and his enemies might take that as proof they were right. The Bible often speaks of death as sleep. See Job 3:13 and 1 Thessalonians 4:14. Death puts out the candle because the dawn has come (an old Indian proverb).

An Affirmation of Trust (13:5-6)

Despite the darkness, the psalmist lived in anticipation of the dawn. He trusted in God's steadfast love and knew that he would not be disappointed.

He promised to rejoice and to sing to the Lord for answered prayer (v. 6). Despite his loneliness, the psalmist's faith was unshaken. Faith knows that God will have the last word. And faith expects it to be a good word. God gives us our song back. He restores the joy of our salvation.

On the cross, Jesus cried in dereliction (Matt. 27:46). But his last word was one of triumphant faith (John 19:30).

Psalm 14: Foolish Man

The "fool" described in this psalm is not intellectually deficient. A fool may be smart and even clever. A modern description would be of a secular person—one who lives without regard for God, a practical atheist or cynical agnostic. God and spiritual matters simply are not of any concern to such a person.

Secular Man (14:1-4)

The practical atheist may not deny that God exists. He believes, though, that the Lord is not in control of the world. It is as though God made the world but then went off to let it go its way (this is called deism). In such a view, God does not count for much.

The psalmist depicted the Almighty as a kind of divine Diogenes—looking for an honest man (v. 2). God was disappointed, for he could not find one, "no, not one" (v. 3).

Sin is the universal experience of all of us. All humanity is sinful (see Rom. 3:10-12). Why is it that no man, except Jesus, has made the right choices and lived above sin? The poet claimed that these evildoers gobbled up the poor as though they were eating bread. And they did not pray (v. 4).

God Will Judge (14:5-6)

Those who live without regard for God are in for a surprise! His judgment will be a time of terror, but God will take care of those who trust in him.

Prayer for Restoration (14:7)

This verse sounds like a prayer which would fit the period of the Exile even better than the time of David. Surely, those in captivity longed for the restoration of the fortunes of God's people.

The Repeated Psalm

This psalm and Psalm 53 are almost identical. The two may be different versions of the same song. It describes selfishness and is true of human nature in every generation. There are far more practical atheists than theoretical ones. Caution! We should not live as though God were dead and we were in complete charge of human affairs.

We, too, should pray for God's deliverance from pride and for the restoration of the relationship broken by our sin.

Psalm 15: Guests of God

This psalm was used by Jewish pilgrims entering the Temple to worship. They would ask the question in verse 1 at the entrance. From inside the Temple courtyard, priests would answer (vv. 2-5).

The Question (15:1)

The question in verse 1 is more inclusive than worship. It is as large as life: what kind of persons can come into the presence of God? The answer given is highly ethical, applying to both prayer and life-style. The ethics of the psalms must have had profound influence on the later prophets of the eighth century BC.

"Thy tent" was the earlier tabernacle in the wilderness. "Thy holy hill" was Mount Zion on which the Temple was built in Jerusalem. Both represented the presence of the Almighty on earth. The worshiper was considered the guest of God, enjoying divine hospitality. (Compare Ps. 23:5-6, where the Lord is portrayed as the psalmist's host.)

The Qualifications (15:2-5a)

The list in this psalm is not exhaustive but representative of the high ethical demands of the Ten Commandments.

1. The first requirement is that the believer have *integrity*. He lives blamelessly—doing the right thing and speaking the truth (v. 2). Both his words and deeds show him to be rightly related to God.

2. The godly person is also *considerate*, no idle gossip or slanderer, whose words do not "wander about on his tongue." He is a true friend and considerate of his neighbor (v. 3).

3. The worshiper has the *right perspective*. As a keen judge, he will not applaud a scoundrel but encourages "those who fear the Lord" (v. 4a).

4. He is also *consistent* and a person of his word. Once he gives his word, he will stick by it, even if it proves to be costly. He can be depended upon (v. 4b).

5. The person welcome in God's presence is a *good steward*. He does not make money dishonestly and will not take a bribe (v. 5b). He is not greedy, charging high interest to a brother who must borrow in a time of great need (Ex. 22:25). Banking was unknown in ancient times. Persons are of greater value than things (see Matt. 12:12). Therefore, they are not to be exploited for a profit.

The Reward of the Upright (15:5c)

The person who lives by such a high ethical standard is secure in his relationship with God.

Thus we get a glimpse of the ethical demands on those who worship and live with the Lord. They are expected to be persons of sincerity, consideration, perception, reliability, compassion, and fairness—a tall order! (See 1 John 4:19-21.)

Psalm 16: God, My Heritage

This psalm of confident trust celebrates the joy of God's presence. It begins with a prayer which turns quickly into a confession of faith (vv. 1-2).

One True God (16:1-4)

The Hebrews were always up against the temptation to serve other gods, along with the Lord. The psalmist would not fall for that. He refused to compromise his worship. "The saints" are the holy ones, those who are set apart by God. They are not perfect, but they are dedicated to God. Those who serve pagan deities are bound to be disappointed. (The same is true of moderns who put their trust in such "false gods" as materialism.)

Happiness Is Living in Fellowship with God (16:5-8)

The psalmist's "portion" and "cup" were his heritage from God. He found this spiritual relationship pleasant and satisfying (v. 6). How blessed are those who serve the Lord. They have happiness the world cannot even imagine.

The psalmist sang about having divine counsel and instruction. He could rest at night, knowing he was secure in the Lord (vv. 7-8).

Joy in the Lord (16:9-11)

The psalmist's whole person rejoiced in the Lord—heart, soul, and body (v. 9). This relationship gave him both security and joy.

God spared him from death. (Sheol and the Pit or grave are synonymous—the abode of the dead.) More than that, the psalmist was given a purposeful life and "fulness of joy" (v. 11). Peter quoted from this psalm in his sermon on the Day of Pentecost (Acts 2:25-33).

It is questionable whether the psalmist had a view of resurrection and life after death. However, Peter and Paul saw the resurrection of Jesus as the fulfillment of this longing (see Acts 13:35).

Psalm 17: A Cry for Vindication

This is a very emotional prayer. The psalmist was as sure of the presence of God as in Psalm 16. He protested his innocence before false accusers.

A Plea for Justice (17:1-2)

This was his cry for vindication. He wanted God to judge him to be right and his enemies to be wrong. He wanted justice done. He asked God to hear "my plea . . . my cry . . . my prayer" (NEB). This triple appeal shows his sense of urgency.

A Declaration of Innocence (17:3-5)

God had tried the psalmist in a night prayer vigil. He put him to the test, "Thou hast assayed me" (NEB), and found no evil (v. 3). The psalmist had avoided violence and walked faithfully in the right path. This is not a song of self-righteousness. Rather, the poet was answering his accusers.

A Request for Divine Protection (17:6-9)

The psalmist prayed in confidence that God would hear and answer (v. 6). He asked that God demonstrate his covenant love and be his Savior from enemies (v. 7).

Two lovely metaphors of divine protection were used in verse 8. He prayed that God would keep him as "the apple of [his] eye." This is the pupil of the eye which is precious and is carefully guarded. He was not asking God to play favorites and make him a pet. He also prayed to be kept "in the shadow of thy wings." This could refer to the wings of the cherubim in the Temple—that is, in the divine presence. It may be a simple plea for protection, as a hen or eagle protects her chicks beneath her wings.

A Description of His Enemies (17:10-14)

They were pitiless, arrogant, and cruel (vv. 10-11). They were as merciless as a young lion waiting in ambush to take its prey (v. 12).

The poet then gave vent to an emotional outburst against his enemies (vv. 13-14). He asked that they be punished to the third generation (see Ex. 20:5). This is a stern passage in which he asked God to give them what they deserved for their wickedness.

A Note of Assurance (17:15)

The psalm concluded with an expression of confidence. He expected God to act on his behalf in the morning.

We may feel the psalmist's outburst against his enemies to be overly severe. The setting of this psalm was unjust persecution. Remember that these were pre-Christian times. One's personal enemies were considered the enemies of God. Christian history has its bloodstained pages, too. Let us not be quick to judge earlier times. We are to be on guard that we not despise others. It was not until the time of Jesus that people were taught to love their enemies. Try it. It is not easy. In fact, it is impossible without the grace Jesus gives.

Psalm 18: A Royal Thanksgiving

This mighty hymn is also found in 2 Samuel 22. It celebrates King David's victory over his enemies. It was likely sung by succeeding Davidic kings in thanksgiving for other battles won.

Prelude to Praise (18:1-3)

God had been to King David "my strength . . . my rock . . . my fortress . . . my deliverer . . . my shield . . . my stronghold, and my God." With these vivid metaphors, he confessed his faith. The warrior-king looked back over his life and gave God the glory for deliverance and victories.

Gratitude for Divine Deliverance (18:4-30)

The king cried for help (vv. 4-6). He was almost overwhelmed by death. The cords of death were like a net ensnaring him. The torrents or waves almost overwhelmed and destroyed him. God heard the cry "from his temple." By "temple" King David would have meant heaven, where God dwells. Later kings would have seen it as a reference to Solomon's Temple in Jerusalem, as well.

Heaven responded to his plea with a mighty display of power and deliverance (vv. 7-19). God came in power: amid an earthquake (v. 7), fire (v. 8), dark storm clouds (vv. 9-11), and a great storm (vv. 12-15). God was depicted as riding the wind and storm clouds. His arrows were lightning flashes (v. 14). The mighty wind was seen as breath from his nostrils (v. 15). It was so powerful that it could lay bare the seabed.

The powerful storm struck terror in the hearts of pagans. But the psalmist-king saw it as a symbol of God's powerful deliverance. For him, the storm inspired awe and confidence (vv. 16-19).

The king saw God's deliverance as a reward for his moral purity and faithfulness (vv. 20-24). God rewards those who live ethically and punishes those who are crooked and proud (vv. 25-27). God gives measure for measure, both good and bad. You get what you give. We live in a moral universe. This is basic Old Testament belief.

A Hymn Celebrating Victory (18:31-48)

The king readily acknowledged God as the source of his victory, instead of taking personal credit for it. Only the Lord is God (v. 31). This God girded the king and made him as secure as hinds' feet are on the mountain heights. (Hind refers to a surefooted mountain deer.)

The king did his part in battle (vv. 37-38). Yet he felt it was God who gave him the victory over his enemies (vv. 39-41). The end result was that the defeated nations acknowledged the king's sovereignty (vv. 43-45). They paid homage to him.

The king sang his grateful praise to the Lord (vv. 46-48). God had proved to be his rock (his defense) and his salvation.

The King's Doxology (18:49-50)

David promised to sing God's praise among the nations. Paul quoted this verse to show God's purpose as the salvation of the Gentiles (Rom. 15:9).

The psalm concludes on a messianic note (v. 50). The word *anointed* means "messiah." The kings were God's anointed, but the Anointed One was yet to come.

Psalm 19: God's Glory Revealed in Nature and Law

Both the created order and God's Word reveal his purpose for humanity. It is interesting that this psalm speaks of God's general revelation of himself in creation and his special revelation in the Ten Commandments. He speaks with many voices to those who will hear.

This psalm is composed of two poems. The first is very ancient, and the second probably dates from the period after the Exile in Babylon. The first sings of God's glory revealed in the heavens. The second celebrates God's will as revealed in his Word and Law.

God's Glory Revealed in the Heavens (19:1-6)

All creation is silently singing the glory of its Creator. In the psalms God's glory is his burning presence in splendor. It inspires man's adoration and praise. The poet envisioned the stars in the heavens singing around God's throne. They keep telling his glory in unending praise Their praise bubbles forth day and night, like a fountain. All this is done without speech or words. No one hears their chorus, yet their message of praise goes throughout all the world. When one looks at the heavens, they become a reminder of their Maker. (See Rom. 10:18.)

The poet called special attention to the sun, the brightest star in heaven. He said that its brightness is like a bridegroom's radiant joy or an eager athlete ready to demonstrate his strength and endurance, running the heavenly track from horizon to horizon. Nothing on earth escapes its warmth. This passage describes a sort of heavenly Olympic Games.

Note that the psalmist celebrated the glory of the sun and stars. Yet he did not worship them as gods, as did his neighbors in Egypt or Persia. Rather, they were part of creation and were made to glorify their Creator.

God's Glory Revealed in His Word (19:7-13)

The Torah—law, instruction, Word of God—is the expression of his revealed will. The stars can tell us there is a Creator God. The Scriptures reveal what he is like and how he cares for his creation, including mankind.

This section of the psalm was carefully constructed. Verse 7 is a one-line statement of his theme, "The law of the Lord is perfect [complete], reviving the soul." The poet used a number of synonymns in these verses to describe the Law:

1. It is a "testimony" to God's will.
2. Its "precepts" give instructions for ethical living.
3. Its "commandments" let us know what God requires.
4. "Fear" teaches us to have reverence for God.
5. The Law's "ordinances" teach what is true and right.

The Law refreshes the inner man, bringing joy and peace. How precious is God's Law: more desirable than refined gold; sweeter than the best honey (a valued commodity in ancient times).

The psalmist prays that he will be kept from both unintentional and deliberate sins.

A Prayer (19:14)

This lovely invocation has been used in worship for centuries. God is our rock, our protection. He is also our Redeemer, saving us from the tyranny of sin.

Pastors may use verse 14 prior to the sermon as follows:

Preacher: May the words of my mouth . . .

People: And the meditation of our hearts . . .

Both: Be acceptable in thy sight, O Lord, our rock and our redeemer.

Psalm 20: A Prayer for Victory

The setting of this psalm was a royal worship service. A Davidic king was about to go into battle. He prayed and offered sacrifices (v. 3) and received assurance of the Lord's help. (See 1 Sam. 13:8-15.) He, and the nation, needed God's presence and protection.

The People Pray for Their King's Victory (20:1-5)

The people prayed that God would "answer . . . protect . . . help . . . support . . . and remember" their king in battle. The fate of the nation rode with him. They asked that God would accept the king's offerings as a token of his devotion (v. 3).

The "name" of the Lord appears three times in this psalm (vv. 1,5,7). It was no magic formula, assuring success. Rather, the name of God was a symbol of his self-revelation and his presence among his people.

Next, the people prayed that God would grant the king the desire of his heart—victory (v. 4). They anticipated cheering his success and waving banners in the triumphal procession (v. 5).

The Priest Pronounces Assurance of Victory (20:6-8)

In much the same way as an assurance of pardon follows a prayer of repentance, the worship leader proclaims the assurance of victory. The Lord will give help to his anointed (king). Help will come from heaven. Note that in verse 2 support was also to come from the Temple. There is no contradiction here. These are simply two ways of stating the same truth. God was present on Mount Zion, but he was also sovereign over all the universe "from his holy heaven" (v. 6). God is not limited but is universal in his power.

Some might trust in mighty arms—war-horses and chariots. While these are important in battle, it is more important to trust in the name of the Lord (v. 7). To trust in arms alone spells failure (v. 8). Compare Isaiah 31:3.

God Save the King (20:9)

This concluding prayer sums up the theme of the psalm. It is also a prayer for the nation, represented in the person of the king. The singing of this psalm was an occasion for strengthening the people's confidence in God, as well as for asking his help in battle.

Psalm 21: A Thanksgiving for Victory

This psalm is paired with Psalm 20. Both are royal psalms. The first is a prayer for victory in battle. The second is a prayer of thanksgiving for victory granted. Obviously, the application of these psalms is broader and more general than their immediate setting. Because of the reference to the king's crown in verse 3, some commentators take this to be a coronation psalm.

Thanksgiving for Answered Prayer (21:1-7)

God had helped the king (the words for *help* and *salvation* are the same). His "heart's desire" had been granted (v. 2). God had blessed the king with majesty as well as success in battle (v. 3). He had been granted long life (v. 4). This promise of unending life applied to the dynasty and ultimately to the Messiah. The king knew both glory and gladness (vv. 5-6). The basis of his greatness was his trust in God's steadfast love (v. 7). The human side of that equation was *trust*. The divine side was *covenant love*.

Hope of Future Victories (21:8-12)

War with neighboring tribes appeared inevitable for Israel. Thus it was essential that they rely on the Lord. The prayer for the destruction of their enemies' children sounds harsh. It reflects the fearful threat of future wars among people dedicated to vengeance. There seemed to be no thought that enemies could one day become friends. Notice that the nation's enemies were also considered God's enemies.

In verse 9 we probably have the description of a besieged city set on fire with its population still inside ("as a blazing oven"). A broader application of this passage is God's final defeat of evil.

A Shout of Praise (21:13)

This concluding prayer was probably sung by the congregation. It has a future as well as a present reference.

The church uses this psalm in its celebration of Christ's ascension. Christ has defeated the power of evil and has received glory from the Father.

Psalm 22: Agony and Ecstasy

This is one of the most eloquent statements of human anguish in all literature. Yet it concludes with a declaration of faith and praise.

The psalm is a vivid statement of human suffering which describes both physical illness and spiritual despair. The poet's sickness was compounded by his sense of being abandoned by God.

Jesus quoted verse 1 from the cross (Matt. 27:46). His suffering was amazingly parallel to the descriptions in this psalm, which has been called the Passion Psalm. Little wonder that the early church felt the hymn to be prophetic:

He was mocked and scorned by the crowd (vv. 7-8).

He suffered from thirst (v. 15).

His hands and feet were pierced (v. 16).

They divided his clothing at the foot of the cross (v. 18).

The description of his agony is reflected in verses 14-16. This psalm is often used in Christian worship on Good Friday, but it has deep significance for any person who is suffering physical and mental anguish. John Durham says it describes "a movement in experience from hell to heaven."[1]

The Cry of Anguish (22:1-21)

The psalmist experienced the absence of God. But his use of "My God" shows he still had faith (v. 1). His agony persisted day and night (v. 2).

God had delivered his forebears (vv. 3-5). But the psalmist felt worthless and despised (v. 6). Note the vivid description of the mockery: "They make mouths at me, they wag their heads" (v. 7). His enemies were sarcastic (v. 8). The poet appealed to God, who had cared for him from his birth (vv. 9-10).

In verses 12-21 we have four vivid word pictures of the psalmist's torment:

1. In a nightmare description he told about the threat of strong bulls, roaring lions, and wild beasts. Bashan was a fertile pastureland across the Jordan River, noted for its fat cattle and fierce bulls (Amos 4:1).

2. The poet described his sickness unto death (vv. 14-15). He experienced weakness, heart failure, and extreme thirst. He was reduced to a skeleton (v. 17). He was almost laid low in "the dust of death."

3. He was surrounded by fierce enemies, closing in for the kill. They were like a pack of wild dogs (v. 16). Still, he cried out for help from the Lord (vv. 19-21).

4. The greatest agony of all was God's absence or distance from him. This theme was repeated in verses 1, 11, 19. That was the most unbearable thing he had to suffer.

A Hymn of Praise (22:22-31)

The mood of the psalm suddenly changed from painful lament to exalted praise. He vowed to praise God for his deliverance and to call on the congregation to join him in his adoration of the Lord (vv. 22-23). God heard his cry (v. 24). God himself is the author of our praise (v. 25).

With prophetic insight the psalmist looked down the years and glimpsed the coming kingdom of God. He saw distant nations being converted to faith in God (v. 27). Even generations yet unborn would enjoy his salvation (vv. 30-31). This has come to pass.

The psalm of anguish ends on a glad note. Like the psalmist and like Jesus, we, too, ask, "My God, why?" May we also share their faith in the Father.

Note

1. John Durham, "Psalms," *The Broadman Bible Commentary* (Nashville: Broadman Press, 1971), vol. 4, p. 212.

Psalm 23: Our Shepherd—Our Host

This is the psalm of psalms—the favorite of young and old alike. It is one of the best known and most loved passages in the Bible, second only to the Lord's Prayer. Little children memorize it before they learn to read. Aged saints die with its words on their lips.

Psalm 23 is a personal affirmation of faith. It is timeless: so simple a child can understand it, yet so profound no scholar has ever drawn it dry.

Imagine the setting when the shepherd David sang it for the first time. It was a cold, starry night in Judea. The stars seemed so close he felt as though he could reach up and rake them down. The day of grazing and search for water was over. The sheep huddled asleep inside a thornbush and stone enclosure. But the shepherd's work was not done. He had to keep a wary eye open for predatory wild animals.

The campfire embers, fanned by the night breeze, glowed red again. He listened to the ancient sound of a shepherd's reed flute, then a melodic Hebrew song. David's heart raced with joy at the thought of God's presence. These deep feelings overflowed into a psalm. "The Lord is my shepherd." Who would have thought it would be so precious to believers more than three thousand years later?

Psalm 22 is a song of deep anguish. Psalm 24 is a hymn of triumph. The twenty-third Psalm is a bridge over troubled waters, joining the two. It is realistic. It is no sundial, recording only the bright hours. Psalm 23 reminds us that God is with us in the valley of deep darkness as well as in times of joy.

The Lord Is My Shepherd (23:1-4)

This metaphor was a familiar one. (See Ps. 100 and Isa. 40:11.) The patriarchs, as well as Moses and David, were all shepherds. The king was often referred to as the shepherd of his people. This was true even of Egypt's pharaohs. Jesus called himself "the Good Shepherd" and commanded Peter to "feed my sheep."

To call God his Shepherd meant to the psalmist:

1. God *provides* his needs: "I shall not want." As the shepherd provides green pastures and still pools of water, so every good gift is from the hand of the Almighty. This is the basis of stewardship. He gives more than the psalmist's physical needs. God also "restores my soul."

2. God *guides* the psalmist—he leads in the right paths. "For his name's sake" means that the very honor of God is involved in the relationship. We can be sure he is absolutely dependable (v. 3). Jesus said, "I know my own and my own know me" (John 10:14). The word *pastor* comes from the Latin word for *shepherd*. (See 1 Pet. 5:1-4.) We can trust a benevolent divine Providence.

3. God *comforts* and protects the psalmist (v. 4). Note that he spoke about walking *through* the valley of the shadow of death. Death is a passage, not a dead end. Every exit is also an entrance. The shepherd's rod or club and staff were stern weapons. Yet the psalmist felt comforted because they were used for his protection. Thus he could be free of fear—even in times of great danger. Christians know that not even the last enemy, death, can hold any ultimate terror for those whose trust is in the risen Christ.

This psalm is no sleepy pastoral depicting spiritual stagnation. It is the affirmation of faith on the part of one who is on pilgrimage, en route with God. "The Lord is my shepherd" here and now.

The Lord Is My Host (23:5-6)

The psalm changes metaphors at verse 5. The poet spoke of *walking* with his Shepherd in verses 1-4. Then he wrote of *dwelling* with his host in verses 5-6. That can be taken as a future reference.

Note also that the psalm began by referring to God in the third person ("the Lord, [he] is my shepherd"). Then there was a shift to usage of the second person ("thou art with me"). We use the second person only to speak of someone who is present.

To call God his host meant:

1. God provides *gracious hospitality*. The psalmist envisioned himself as the guest of God at a banquet. This was a foreshadowing of the Lord's Supper and the messianic banquet in heaven (Rev. 19:9). According to Oriental custom, the host would guarantee the safety of the psalmist, even in the presence of his enemies.

Note the generosity of God as host. He anoints his guest's head and beard with perfumed oil. The psalmist's cup brims over with overflowing abundance. God is extravagant in his blessings and not stingy. He gives both our necessities and many extras.

2. God is anxious to *bless*. He is no reluctant deity who must be badgered to give his favors. Divine "goodness and mercy" pursue the psalmist. An unknown Scottish preacher said of this text: "The Lord is my Shepherd, aye, and more than that, he has two fine collie dogs, 'goodness and mercy.' And they will see me safely home."

3. To "*dwell* in the house of the Lord forever" is a poetic way of saying the psalmist will be with God. This is the climax of the psalm. The most beautiful promise of heaven is that we will enjoy the presence of God forever.

Jesus obviously knew and loved this psalm. He applied it to himself and his mission (John 10). In Christian theology, Jesus was both the Good Shepherd and the sacrificial Lamb of God. He cares for his sheep, and he gave himself for them—to take away the sin of the world. David would have never thought of that.

Psalm 24: Nature, Man, and God

Worship could be highly dramatic in Israel. Pilgrims coming to the city of Jerusalem for a festival would march in procession. As they came round the Mount of Olives, the sight of the Holy City and its Temple could be breathtaking. (See Ezek. 40:5-16.) Crossing the Kidron Valley, the procession would halt at the gate to the Temple courtyard. This psalm was sung antiphonally with the choir outside asking, "Who is the

King of glory?" The priests within would reply, "The Lord of hosts, he is the King of glory." Some commentators suggest that the procession carried the ark of the covenant. However, this is not stated in the Old Testament.

Nature: The World About Us (24:1-2)

These verses celebrate God's creation of the natural world. It is a place of complicated ecological balance and beauty. It can also be fierce and troubled by fierce storms. This beautiful and fierce world reflects its Creator.

The ancient view of the world was of a saucer floating on the waters of the sea. The psalm reflects that understanding.

Man: The World Within (24:3-6)

The thought here is similar to that in Psalm 15—who is worthy to come into the presence of the Lord and worship (v. 3)? Priests answer from within the Temple area. The worshiper should be a person of integrity. He is to be pure in hand and heart—in action and intention. Both his motives and his deeds are to be right. He is to be neither proud nor deceitful (v. 4).

God will bless and vindicate such persons (v. 5). The pilgrims who have come to worship are considered a worthy "generation" (v. 6).

God: The World Beyond (24:7-10)

The choir with the procession poetically addressed the Temple gates (v. 7). Voices of priests from within would reply, "Who is the King of glory?" This dialogue is both poetic and has a teaching value. Imagine children and youth in the procession listening to these questions and answers.

The choir's response is surprising. They reply that he is "the Lord, mighty in battle" (a warrior God); and he is "the Lord of hosts" (armies). This is a poetic way of speaking of the Lord as a God of might and great power. Israel felt that the Lord led their armies to victory in battle. This term, "the Lord of hosts," occurs more than 250 times in the Old Testament.

God is eternal (Ps. 118:1), holy, and mighty. He is "the King of glory!" (v. 10). His work is that of creator and Redeemer. Nature glorifies its Maker. Man is meant to respond to him in worship and gratitude. This psalm is a dramatic portrayal of Israel's worship.

Psalm 25: A Prayer of Trust and Lament

Psalm 25 is an acrostic. Each verse begins with a different letter of the Hebrew alphabet. Because of this, its thought does not flow smoothly. Its themes are trust in God, a plea for divine guidance, and prayer for forgiveness.

Prayer for Protection, Guidance, and Pardon (25:1-7)

The psalm begins with the poet's assertion of trust in God (vv. 1-2). Repeatedly, he asked that he not be "put to shame" in the presence of his enemies.

The psalmist prayed for the Lord's guidance and leading (vv. 4-5). He asked that God remember his mercy and not remember his sins (vv. 6-7). Two words are used for his wrongdoing: *sins* are youthful, moral failures; *transgressions* are deliberate acts of rebellion.

God's Goodness, Fairness, and Faithfulness (25:8-15)

God is upright and instructs sinners in the right way to live (v. 8). His steadfast love causes him to keep his covenant with his chosen ones (vv. 9-10). God acts with justice. The psalmist renewed his prayer to be forgiven (v. 11). He longed to enjoy the "friendship of the Lord" (vv. 12-15).

Prayers for Deliverance (25:16-21)

In his loneliness, the psalmist asked for divine grace (vv. 15-16). The word translated *forgive* means to lift a burden—an apt description of guilt and forgiveness.

Note verse 21, "May integrity and uprightness preserve me." This is not a case of self-righteousness. Rather, these are the characteristics of one who is in right relationship with God.

The final verse is a prayer for the nation. It has been appended to the personal prayer which makes up the body of the psalm. This made it more useful in public worship.

To trust in God is the main emphasis of Psalm 25.

Psalm 26: Vindicate the Innocent

The psalmist had been accused of wrongdoing. He protested that he was innocent and went to the Temple, seeking vindication. (See 1 Kings

8:31-32.) He did not claim to be sinless, but declared himself innocent of the charges brought against him. He appealed for justice based on his integrity.

This psalm is similar to Psalms 7 and 17 and is a companion to Psalm 28. It is quite old, predating the Exile.

A Plea for Vindication (26:1-3)

The psalmist had been loyal to God, with a life-style of personal integrity. His faith and trust in God was unshaken. Thus he could pray for justice. He asked that God would prove, try, and test him in heart and mind—in the inner man.

A Plea of Innocence (26:4-7)

The worshiper insisted that he had refrained from running with the wrong crowd. He did not consort with the wicked (vv. 4-5). In a ritual to symbolize his innocence, he washed his hands before the Lord (v. 6). Recall Pilate's action following the trial of Jesus (Matt. 27:24). Ritual washing of one's hands before worship was customary as a symbol of purity (Ex. 30:17-21).

Next, he went around the altar with a procession, singing about God's mighty acts (v. 7).

A Plea of Devotion (26:8-12)

The psalmist loved God's house where God's glory dwelled (v. 8). God's glory is his revealed presence symbolized by the ark and mercy seat (Ex. 33:18-22). The psalmist was comfortable with God and could trust him to judge fairly.

He asked to be spared the fate of the wicked, including premature death (vv. 9-10). He felt secure, "on level ground," before the Lord (v. 12).

In this hymn the poet was not bragging about his spiritual virtue; rather, he was giving his personal testimony. He was attesting to his faith and loyalty to God.

Psalm 27: Conquering Fear

There are two distinct moods reflected here. The first six verses constitute an affirmation of faith. Verses 7-14 are a lament and prayer for help. Both reflect the poet's trust in God.

No one is immune to fear. Many fears are healthy and keep us away from danger. Other fears are unhealthy phobias which threaten our faith in the Father.

The Psalmist Declared His Faith (27:1-3)

The poet trusted in the Lord and discovered that he need have no ultimate fear (v. 1). God was his light, his salvation, his stronghold. The light of God dispels the dark of fear and gives quiet confidence. The psalmist said that he would not be afraid even if a whole army threatened him (v. 3). Compare the account of Gideon (Judg. 6:16) and Isaiah (37:6-35).

The psalm reflects the author's personal experience with the Lord. It is his testimony. As a student, John R. Mott read forty-three books about prayer but still had doubts. Then he tried the experience of prayer and was convinced of its effectiveness.[1] This psalm grew out of the firsthand religious experience of the psalmist.

The Psalmist Described His Life with the Lord (27:4-12)

His great desire was the privilege of worship in God's house (compare v. 4 with Ps. 23:6). He enjoyed worship and felt secure in the divine presence. He also found guidance when he would "inquire in his temple" (v. 4). God protects those who trust in him (v. 5). They bring their offerings of gratitude and sing God's praise "with shouts of joy" (v. 6).

Beginning with verse 7, the psalmist began his plea to have his prayer heard. This passage is a study in the anatomy of prayer:[2]

1. God invites the worshiper to seek his face (v. 8).
2. Believers are completely dependent on God's favor (v. 9).
3. Though all others forsake the psalmist, God never will (v. 10).
4. A prayer of humble submission (v. 11).
5. A confession of the psalmist's need (v. 12).

The Difference Faith Made in the Psalmist's Life (27:13-14)

He was not overcome by his fears but trusted in the goodness of the Lord. He expected to see God's goodness in his own lifetime (v. 13).

The closing verse of the psalm is a great admonition based on solid religious experience, "Wait for the Lord!"

Notes

1. Leonard Griffith, *God in Man's Experience* (Waco: Word Books, 1968), p. 42.
2. Ibid., p. 44.

Psalm 28: A Cry for Help

Here we have a personal lament which turns into an answered prayer. It is a companion to Psalm 26, which is a prayer for justice, while Psalm 28 is an appeal for mercy. Both psalms plead for deliverance and focus on the Temple as a symbol of God's saving presence.

A Cry for Help (28:1-5)

The psalmist felt keenly the absence of God. His prayers were met with silence. The Pit in verse 1 is a synonym for Sheol, the abode of the dead.

He lifted up his hands in prayer, facing the holy of holies in the Temple, where God was present (v. 2). The characteristic stance for prayer among the Hebrews was standing, lifting one's hands, palms up, toward heaven. Kneeling, bowing, and folding one's hands in prayer dates from medieval times.

The poet prayed that the moral law of the universe might prevail, giving the wicked what they deserve (vv. 4-5). He asked that he be spared their fate (v. 3).

Answered Prayer (28:6-7)

A dramatic change occurs in the mood of the psalm at verse 6. The author began to praise God for hearing and answering his prayer. His plea gave way to adoration, an expression of his faith and gratitude.

Prayer for the Nation (28:8-9)

The focus shifts from the psalmist to the nation in these verses. God is the "strength" and "refuge" of his people (v. 8). The last verse is a series of short petitions: "Save thy people . . . bless thy heritage . . . be their shepherd . . . carry them forever."

Some people's religion is a burden of rules and prohibitions which they must bear. Biblical faith is a relationship with God in which he bears us. It is not burdensome. John Durham reminds us that the great lesson of this psalm is "that it is God who must be sought first of all, and not deliverance."[1]

Note

1. John Durham, "Psalms," *The Broadman Bible Commentary* (Nashville: Broadman Press, 1971), vol. 4, p. 228.

Psalm 29: The Voice of God in Nature

This psalm is one of the most majestic and dramatic poems in the Psalter. It is believed to be very ancient, as well. In Psalms 8 and 19 the authors were aware of the presence of God in nature—in the calm night sky. This psalmist experienced God in the fury of a thunderstorm.

Israel is a dry land where it does not rain for months each year. Then in the autumn, clouds come in from the Mediterranean Sea bringing welcome rain. This psalm could have been used in worship, celebrating the return of these life-giving rainstorms.

Let the Angels Join in Worship (29:1-2)

The psalmist summoned the angelic host surrounding God's throne to join in worship. They were called to ascribe glory to God, while human worshipers did the same in his Temple on earth. Heaven and earth unite in his praise.

The Voice of God in the Storm (29:3-9)

Seven times the poet wrote of "the voice of the Lord," suggesting seven peals of thunder (see Ps. 18:13; Job 37:2-5; Rev. 10:3). Note the dramatic effects of the fierce storms:

1. It covered the entire Holy Land from snowcapped Mount Hermon and Mount Lebanon in the north to Kadesh and the wilderness in the south.

2. God was in control of "the waters" of the deep (vv. 3-4). At creation he brought order out of chaos (Gen. 1:1-10).

3. The voice of the Lord rebuked the proud cedars and mountains of Lebanon (vv. 5-6). His storm splintered the old cedars and made the mountains "skip" in terror before the Lord. *Sirion* is the Phoenician name for Mount Hermon.

4. The voice of the Lord and lightning ("flames of fire") from the storm stirred up the wilderness (vv. 7-8). The worshiper would be reminded of the thunder and lightning on Mount Sinai when the Law was given to Moses (Ex. 19:16). Wind and fire are also associated with the coming of God's Spirit on Pentecost (Acts 2:1-4).

5. The storm left its mark on the forest (v. 9). The effect of the storm was not to frighten God's people, but to elicit their praise—"and in his temple all cry, 'Glory!' " Those who worship God in heaven and on earth are united in spontaneous praise (v. 1 speaks of the angels' worship and v. 9 of human adoration).

The Calm After the Storm (29:10-11)

God was in control of the flood and the storm. (The Hebrew word used here for *flood* is used in Gen. 6—11 of Noah's flood.) Ancient pagans, such as the Babylonians, thought the gods themselves were frightened and threatened by the flood. Therefore, God could give his people strength and peace because he controlled the rainstorms.

The storm was glorious to the people because it demonstrated God's power and his provision of rain. We, too, are equally dependent on God and can see his power and beauty in nature—calm and fierce.

Psalm 30: Joy in the Morning

This is a hymn of thanksgiving for healing. It was used in public worship, for it asks that other believers join in praise to God (v. 4).

The Psalmist's Thanksgiving (30:1-5)

The poet was critically ill (v. 2). His death would have pleased his enemies (v. 1). In his distress he cried out to God. The Almighty heard his prayer and healed him, drawing him up from the verge of death. The Lord restored his health (v. 3). The psalmist praised the Lord and invited others to join him in thanksgiving (v. 4).

Verse 5 is a lovely text. The psalmist considered his suffering a sign of God's "anger," due to his sin. He was confident that the divine displeasure would be temporary. It would be replaced by God's favor, which would last throughout his lifetime. Then he contrasted tears and joy. He cried through the night of suffering. But "joy comes with the morning." Such a thought has brought great comfort to those who suffer. Christians find here a hope that earthly suffering will one day be replaced by heavenly joy. Heaven is a place where there are no tears, no more pain, no suffering. The night of crying is contrasted with the morning's joy. Weeping is temporary, but joy is enduring.

The Psalmist's Testimony (30:6-12)

Prior to his illness the poet had enjoyed prosperity and felt both secure and self-sufficient (v. 6). It is easy to feel quite confident as long as everything is going well. We may even be tempted to be cocky and proud, thinking that good health and affluence are things we deserve—that having them is our right.

Suddenly everything changed for the psalmist. In his illness the Lord seemed far away. He was at the point of panic (v. 7). He began to pray earnestly (v. 8). He tried to reason with the Lord, maybe even to strike a bargain with him (v. 9). After all, if he died and returned to dust, he could no longer serve and praise the Lord.

His prayer took on a new dimension at verse 10. He prayed in complete reliance on God's grace—not on the basis of what he felt he deserved.

At that point, God heard and granted his request for healing and help. In happy response he declared that God had turned his somber sackcloth of sorrow into bright garments of gladness. He went from mourning to joy (vv. 11-12). In his exultation he promised to "give thanks to thee for ever."

In the course of the poet's experience his understanding of God and his faith were strengthened. He moved from an attitude of self-sufficiency (v. 6), to bargaining with God (v. 9), to utter dependence on divine grace (v. 10). This is a normal progression often seen in maturing religious experience. Note that he did not fail to give thanks for his deliverance, as many do. (Recall Jesus healing ten lepers.)

Prosperous churches may find a lesson here, as well. If they become self-assured, they can forget their dependence on God and lose his power. Never fail to give God the glory for every achievement.

Psalm 31: Into Thy Hands

One of the ingenious characteristics of the Psalms is that they can be both highly personal and yet appropriate for public worship, as well. Their message is timeless, having been used and treasured across the ages.

The structure of this psalm alternates between lament and thanksgiving, between a plea for help and praise of God's goodness. Some have thought it the blending of two different psalms. More likely, it is simply an expression of the tension between times of trouble and trust in God. The poet's expressions of his needs are quite elaborate. They include: danger in battle, illness, loneliness, threat, persecution, and ensnaring enemies.

The golden text of this psalm is verse 5: "Into thy hand I commit my spirit."

A Cry for Deliverance (31:1-18)

The psalmist began with a testimony of his trust in God. God had been his refuge in past times of trouble (v. 1). He asked that he would be his mountain fortress now and in the future (v. 2). The Judean hill country was a place of safety in a time of invasion or similar danger. Recall David fleeing King Saul in that region.

The poet's enemies were out to trap him as a hunter ensnares an animal or bird (v. 4). This theme is often repeated in the Psalms (see 9:15; 35:7; 57:6; 140:5).

"Into thy hand I commit my spirit" was the psalmist's prayer of trust in the presence of his enemies (v. 5). How appropriate that Jesus' last words from the cross were this prayer of faith. Note that he added the personal address, "Father" (Luke 23:46).

In verse 7 we have a further statement of the poet's confidence in God's trustworthy love. Though his enemies had him in a tight place, he believed God would set his feet "in a broad place" (v. 8).

A Lament (31:9-18)

The psalmist next described his "distress" in greater detail. He was filled with grief (v. 9) and depressed (v. 10). He suffered the scorn of his enemies (v. 11) and felt as forgotten as the dead. He was as useless as a broken clay pot (v. 12). His enemies carried out a campaign of whispers against him, plotting to kill him (v. 13). Far from his having paranoia, this may literally have been the case.

Even in this plight, the psalmist's trust in God was not shaken: "Thou art my God" (v. 14) and "My times are in thy hand" (v. 15). God was in control of his destiny. These are powerful affirmations of faith. He prayed that he might not be put to shame, but that his enemies would (v. 17).

A Thanksgiving (31:19-24)

Divine goodness is not stingy but "abundant" (compare Ps. 23:5). This favor and protection is available to all who trust in the Lord (vv. 19-20). Finally, the psalmist called on all believers to "love the Lord . . . be strong . . . take courage and . . . wait (depend) for the Lord" (vv. 23-24).

Psalm 32: The Joy of Forgiveness

Note that this psalm begins with a beatitude, "Happy is the man

whose disobedience is forgiven, whose sin is put away!" (v. 1, NEB).
Such a person is to be congratulated, indeed. This is the second of the
penitential psalms used in Christian worship (6; 32; 38; 51; 102; 130;
143). Psalm 32 is also a song of thanksgiving and a wisdom poem. It
was the favorite psalm of Augustine, who placed a copy of it on the wall
beside his bed.

The Joy of Forgiveness (32:1-2)

Here the poet used significant words for sin. "Transgression" is deliberate disobedience to God's known will. "Sin" is a general term which
means moral failure, literally missing the mark. "Iniquity" signifies
crooked and perverse qualities.

The psalmist used equally powerful words to describe divine forgiveness: His sins were "forgiven" or literally lifted as a burden from the
shoulders—they were "rolled away." His crimes were "covered" by the
divine Judge—"case dismissed." Finally, he wrote that "the Lord imputes
no iniquity." This means he cancels the sin debt on heaven's ledger.

Note that the apostle Paul quoted these verses when writing about
justification (Rom. 4:7-8). The psalm sounds a call to repentance, citing
the joy of one whose sins have been forgiven. But God pardons only
those who confess their sins, as we shall see in the following verses.

The Burden of Guilt (32:3-4)

There had been a time when the psalmist refused to acknowledge his
sin (v. 3). The resulting guilt became an unbearable burden. It made the
poet literally ill and depressed. He came under conviction for his sins—
"Thy hand was heavy upon me" (v. 4). A guilty conscience can have dire
consequences, physical and emotional.

Sin Confessed and Forgiven (32:5)

Once the psalmist acknowledged his sin and quit trying to hide it, he
experienced divine forgiveness. Confession is good for the soul. Of
course, God already knew about his sin. Confession meant that the poet
decided to give up his self-deceit. To his great relief, God lifted his burden of guilt and gave his song back.

A Witness from Experience (32:6-9)

He called on others to pray also when they found themselves in distress (v. 6). He praised God for protecting and guarding him (v. 7).

Next, the psalmist instructed others in the right way (v. 8). He urged them not to be as stubborn as a mule, which sometimes can only be checked with bit and bridle (v. 9).

A Call to Rejoice (32:10-11)

Here the author contrasted the lot of the wicked and that of the righteous who are surrounded by steadfast love (v. 10). Grace envelops those who trust God. In the final verse he sounded a threefold call to joy: "Be glad . . . rejoice . . . and shout for joy."

The psalm teaches the importance of being honest with God. The poet tried to hide his guilt but found it to be unbearable. He found that honesty is the best policy in spiritual matters, as well.

Psalm 33: God's Work and Word

The setting of this psalm is the congregation at worship. It is an impressive hymn of praise. The structure of the psalm expresses many aspects of worship such as adoration, celebration, and dedication.

Call to Worship (33:1-3)

The faithful are invited to praise the Lord with the lyre and harp. These are representative of musical instruments used to accompany congregational singing. A more complete list of ancient musical instruments used in worship is found in Psalm 150.

The "new song" in verse 3 may refer to this new psalm. Or it may reflect the spiritual renewal which is often experienced in worship.

God's Creative Word (33:4-9)

The Lord created the heavens by his word (v. 6). In verse 4 his "word" and "work" are parallel. The poet characterized the divine activity as being upright, faithful, just, and loving.

Verse 7 refers to the original creation in which God set the limits of the sea and underground water. "Bottle" is a container such as a goatskin (NEB). Here and in verse 6 we have a reflection of Genesis 1. God's creative power inspires reverence and awe among mankind (vv. 8-9). His power is such that he appears to create effortlessly.

God's Plan and Purpose (33:10-12)

God not only made the world, but he also continues to care about it. He is involved with his creation and his creatures. The plans of the nations don't amount to much, but the purpose of God determines the outcome of history (vv. 10-11). In verse 12 we have a ringing beatitude and benediction: "Blessed is the nation whose God is the Lord." This is an appropriate text for a patriotic observance.

God's Providential Care (33:13-19)

God watches over people. He is not detached and disinterested like the Greek gods. He observes people's actions and knows what is in their hearts (their intentions). The Almighty is at work in history as surely as he was at work in creation.

"The eye of the Lord" in verse 18 is a way of speaking of divine providence. The destiny of people and nations is in his hands. Believers are under his watchful care (vv. 18-19).

Sovereign God, Our Basis of Hope (33:20-22)

The psalm began with joyous praise. It ended on the note of joyous trust. It called for patient dependence on the Lord (v. 20). Next, the psalm reminded the worshiper to "trust in his holy name" (v. 21). Finally, it issued an invitation to "hope" in the Lord, due to his "steadfast love" (v. 22). This section summarizes the message of the psalm.

God is the sovereign Lord of both creation and history (see Rom. 8:25).

Psalm 34: Taste and See That the Lord Is Good

Here we have a companion psalm to Psalm 25. Both are acrostic. This means each verse begins with the succeeding letter of the Hebrew alphabet. Psalm 25 is a lament, and Psalm 34 is a thanksgiving and an invitation to try faith in God. They are both what is called "Wisdom Literature" and have a teaching purpose.

Invitation to Gratitude (34:1-7)

The psalmist praised the Lord and invited other worshipers to join in his joy (vv. 1-3). He boasted about the faithfulness of God (compare 1 Cor. 1:31).

The Lord "delivered" the psalmist from fear, trouble, and affliction (vv. 4,17,19). The word literally means the Lord "snatched" him from danger at the last moment. Therefore, instead of his blushing with shame, his face was radiant, glowing at his fellowship with the Lord (v.

5). The poor and oppressed are saved by the Lord (v. 6). And the "angel of the Lord" protects those who have reverence (fear) for God (v. 7). The angel of the Lord is his messenger who represents the Lord himself (see Ex. 23:20; Judg. 6:11-23).

Invitation to Experience (34:8-14)

To "taste" is to know by personal experience, firsthand. Verse 8 is often used in the observance of the Lord's Supper. The psalmist invited others to try God for themselves. That is the ultimate proof.

The "fear of the Lord" is an Old Testament way of describing reverence (v. 9). "Saints" are believers. God provides for them (v. 10). In this part of the psalm the poet took the role of a teacher instructing his students, "sons" (v. 11), on the theme of reverence. This passage is similar to Proverbs 1—9. Reverence is intended to issue in ethical conduct.

In verse 12 we have a summary of reverence. He who wants to live a long time should refrain from speaking deceitfully, turn from wrong and do what is right, and seek those things which lead to peace. First Peter 3:10-12 quotes verses 12-16 from this psalm. The reason New Testament quotations from the Old are not exact is that the New Testament writers were using a Greek translation of the Old Testament. It was called the Septuagint. Our English translations of the Old Testament are based on the Hebrew text.

The Justice and Nearness of God (34:15-22)

Note the vivid metaphors used of God in verses 15-16: "the eyes of the Lord . . . his ears . . . the face of the Lord." The psalmist taught that the Lord cares for the righteous but cuts off the remembrance of the wicked. He is the deliverer of the righteous (vv. 17,19). Evil contains the seed of its own destruction (v. 21). But God redeems and forgives those who trust in him (v. 22). He ransoms his own, paying their sin debt.

Psalm 35: Trouble Comes in Threes

An old saying has it that "trouble comes in threes." The author of Psalm 35 might well agree. It is a threefold lament. Each plea for deliverance concluded with a brief thanksgiving for divine help (vv. 10,18,28). Some commentators think that Psalm 35 is a composite of three different psalms. It is similar to Psalm 7. The enemies here may be personal, or they may be rival states who challenge the king's authority. The poem is a cry for vindication. It is highly emotional, expressing both hurt and anger. The poet is convinced both of his own innocence and of God's power to set the record straight.

"Contend, O Lord" (35:1-10)

Here we have the vivid poetic imagery of battle. The Lord is pictured as fighting on behalf of the psalmist. His enemies are God's enemies (v. 1). He asked that they be put to shame, confounded and driven before the angel of the Lord like chaff before the wind (vv. 4-5). (Compare Ps. 1:4.)

Without provocation the psalmist's enemies had set nets and dug a pit to ensnare him. He asks that they fall prey to their own traps (vv. 7-8).

In verses 9-10 the poet vowed to rejoice and praise God for his deliverance. "O Lord, who is like thee?" is a phrase of adoration. Consider the uniqueness of God. He alone is Creator, Sustainer, and our heavenly Father. There is no one else in the universe who has his limitless power and love.

"How Long, O Lord?" (35:11-18)

In the second lament "malicious witnesses" attack the psalmist's reputation. They accused him of crimes of which he hadn't even heard—purely fabrications.

The irony of the situation is not their wickedness as much as their *ingratitude*. When they were ill, he had done everything possible to help them. He wore sackcloth and fasted. He grieved and prayed for them as one would for a brother or for his own mother (vv. 13-14). Yet when the poet became ill or found himself in trouble, these same persons "gathered in glee." They slandered and mocked him.

Ingratitude from those we have helped is a bitter pill to swallow. As Shakespeare said, it is "sharper than a serpent's tooth" (*King Lear*, II, iv, 312). We should help others without expecting to be thanked, but we should always remember to be grateful to all who have helped us.

In exasperation the psalmist cried out, "How long, O Lord?" and pleaded for rescue (v. 17). In the final verse of this section the refrain of praise appears again (v. 18).

"Vindicate Me, O Lord" (35:19-28)

The third time the poet lamented his enemies. They winked at one another knowingly and hated him without reason (v. 19). They were not men of peace like the "quiet in the land" (v. 20). Rather, they were contemptuous and deceitful. Like children, they made fun of him, saying, "Aha, aha!" (v. 21).

The psalmist prayed for God to come to his aid—to vindicate him in the sight of his enemies (vv. 22-24). He wanted them discredited (v. 26).

The psalm concludes with its third refrain of praise (v. 28). The psalmist reminds us that men can be vicious and ungrateful. However, the three prayers of praise at the conclusion of each stanza show his faith that God will provide a solution to his dilemma (see Ps. 4). This kind of faith was beautifully exemplified by Jesus in the garden of Gethsemane (Matt. 26:36-46).

Psalm 36: Wickedness of Man—Goodness of God

The wickedness of man is used as a foil for the goodness of God in this psalm. The character of God is contrasted with the sinfulness of man. In the title David is called "the servant of the Lord" (see 1 Sam. 23:10-11).

Thus Says Sin (36:1-4)

The prophets often began their message with, "Thus says the Lord." In a startling fashion the psalmist began by saying, in effect, "Thus says transgression."

Evil is personified here as a demonic spirit. It "whispers" to the heart of wicked persons, telling them they have nothing to fear from God. Satan is the "Father of Lies." Paul quoted the last half of the first verse in his description of human depravity (Rom. 3:18). The ungodly person asks, "Who is to know?" He thinks God will not care or find out what he is up to (v. 2).

The wicked flatter themselves to make themselves look good in their own eyes. They hate to admit they are wrong. Evil is easily rationalized, at least for a time. These persons live like blindfolded people in a world of illusion. Their mouths are filled with deceit (v. 3) and their lives with mischief rather than good (v. 4). The end result is self-deception. They certainly do not fool God. Thinking they are a law to themselves, they will discover that they are slaves to an evil master who will eventually destroy them.

The Goodness of God (36:5-9)

Against the backdrop of humanity's evil desires and actions, the psalmist sang of the righteousness of God. The worshiper is reminded of

God's steadfast love, righteousness, protection, and provision.

1. God's *steadfast love* can be counted on (vv. 5,7). He is faithful when all others fail us. Thus his love is precious (compare Ps. 57:10; 108:4). His love reaches from the lofty mountain peaks to the unfathomable depths of the sea. It is both immeasurable and inexhaustible.

2. God is *righteous* and his judgments are fair (v. 6). (See Gen. 1:6; 7:11; Rom. 11:33.) He cares for both people and animals. God is completely dependable; few things are.

3. We benefit from God's *protection.* Poetically, the psalmist stated that persons can "take refuge in the shadow of thy wings" (v. 7). Compare Psalms 17:8; 57:1; 63:7. We are safe and secure with the Lord, with no ultimate fears.

4. God *provides* generously for his own (vv. 8-9). He gives us all we need and more, "abundance" and "the river of thy delights." (See Pss. 65:9-13; 23:5-6.) We enjoy the bounty of our generous host. Think of all the delightful things the Lord has provided for our well-being. The Hebrew word for *delights* is *Eden*, with its river and garden paradise (Gen. 2:10). Compare Jeremiah 2:13 on the fountain of life (v. 9).

God is the source of our life (Jer. 2:13) and our light (John 1:14). "The Lord is my light and my salvation; whom shall I fear?" (Ps. 27:1a).

A Closing Prayer (36:10-12)

In this concluding prayer the psalmist asked for God's continued steadfast love and his salvation from the wickedness of others. Note the vivid figures, "the foot of arrogance" and "the hand of the wicked" (v. 11).

To "know" the Lord (v. 10) means to commit oneself to him and to live in faithful relationship with him (see Isa. 1:1-4). Life and purpose come from God. Humanity alone left to its own devices is pathetic.

Psalm 37: Wisdom in Capsule Form

This poem is a collection of wise sayings by an elder to his students. It is in the form of an acrostic—every other line begins with the succeeding letter of the Hebrew alphabet. Here we find the traditional theology of the Old Testament: the righteous prosper, and the wicked suffer. Its corollary is that suffering is due to sin. Recall how severely Job questioned that point of view. The psalm is made up of a group of twenty proverbs which teach that theology. Suffering is often the result of sin,

but not always. The affliction of the godly posed a real problem for Old
Testament people, as it does for moderns. Their difficulty was greater
than ours, however, because they had no clear idea of life after death
with opportunity for reward and punishment.

"Fret Not . . . Because of the Wicked" (37:1-11)

The wise teacher began by instructing his pupils not to be upset by or
jealous of the prosperity of the wicked. Note how his admonitions rang
out like rifle shots:
- "Trust in the Lord" (v. 3)
- "Delight in the Lord" (v. 4)
- "Commit your way to the Lord" (v. 5)
- "Be still before the Lord" (v. 7)

He insisted that the success of the wicked will be temporary (v. 10).
Taking the long view, the meek shall ultimately possess the land (v. 11;
see Matt. 5:5).

"The Lord Laughs at the Wicked" (37:12-22)

The time of recompense for the wicked is coming (v. 13). They may
plot to destroy the righteous, but their weapons will recoil on them (vv.
14-15). The little which the righteous enjoy is better than the plenty of
the wicked (vv. 16-17). High-handed prosperity, a quick profit, and too-
easy credit will not long succeed (vv. 18-19). By contrast, the righteous
are generous (v. 21). But the wicked are as insubstantial as smoke (v. 20).
Little is much, when God is in it.

God Directs the Steps of the Righteous (37:23-33)

The righteous are not simply left to their own wisdom. Even if they
fall, they will get up again. They may be knocked down, but they are not
knocked out (v. 24).

The experienced poet had never seen the righteous forsaken or his
children begging (vv. 25-26). While there may be exceptions, this is
remarkably true today as well.

"Wait for the Lord" (37:34-40)

Patience is recommended. The elderly appear to have more of this virtue than the young. Those who trust in the Lord find that he helps them,
delivers them, and saves them (v. 40). God takes care of his own. Waiting for the Lord constitutes an act of faith. This is not an easy proverb to

follow since we are such activists. Like Job, we, too, need to learn that it is more important to trust God than to have answers to all our questions.

Psalm 38: Sin and Suffering

The theology of Psalm 37 is expanded here. The poet is convinced that his dreadful suffering is punishment for his sin. The psalm's vivid description of suffering caused the church to make use of it during Holy Week worship. Its theme is similar to the experience of Job, Jeremiah, and Jesus.

Physical Illness (38:1-10)

The psalmist mentioned his physical agony fifteen times in this short poem. He quite openly considered it a punishment from God for his sins; and, repenting, he asked for divine mercy.

The opening of the psalm is very similar to that of Psalm 6. He did not expect to escape punishment for his sin but asked that it be tempered (vv. 1-2). In vivid terms he described his agony of body and soul. His heart throbbed; his strength drained away; and his eyes grew dim (v. 10).

Rejected by Friends and Family (38:11-15)

Persons he thought he could count on kept their distance. They were afraid of being defiled or catching his disease. (See Lev. 13:45-56.) He was an untouchable, ostracized by those dearest to him. The poet did not rebuke them but looked to the Lord for help (vv. 13-15).

Oppressed by His Enemies (38:16-20)

They boasted and rejoiced at his misfortune (v. 16). He did not deserve their enmity (vv. 19-20). But the psalmist did confess his sin to God, casting himself on divine mercy (v. 18).

Appeal for God's Help (38:21-22)

In his utter helplessness the psalmist acknowledged his reliance on God. The poem begins and ends with an appeal to God. (See Ps. 22:1.) The poet trusted God to answer, despite his sin. We can be sure that his prayer was heard. The sinner's prayer of repentance always is.

This psalm depicts profound suffering, the confession of sin, and a prayer for salvation. While we believe that not all suffering is due to sin, still, when trouble comes, we inevitably ask why.

Psalm 39: A Desperate Prayer

What are we to make of death? Psalm 38 deals with the problem of sin and suffering. This psalm portrays the despair of one about to die, with no hope of life afterward. It contains a conversation between the poet and God. He candidly asked the meaning of mankind's brief life and the mystery of death. He tried to be silent (vv. 1-3) but finally had to speak up.

The ancient Israelites had no clear word from God about life after death. Their only idea of immortality seems to have been that a man lives on through his children. "Sheol" was the mysterious abode of the dead—a shadowy land of nothingness, a waste. The real hope and promise of eternal life was accomplished through the resurrection of Jesus Christ.

The Poet Kept Quiet (39:1-3)

He held his peace in the presence of the wicked. He muzzled his mouth and did not ask the ultimate questions burning within him. But his silence did not help. The pain grew worse; his agony increased.

The Poet Spoke Out (39:4-6)

He cried out in anguish. All human effort appeared futile. He could not cure himself and keep death at bay. Life is brief and fleeting at best—only a few "handbreadths" (the width of four fingers). Human life is fragile—a mere breath (vv. 5,11). Even a short life is filled with trouble and turmoil. (Here the poet sounds like the writer of Ecclesiastes.) Man's life is no more than a fleeting shadow (v. 6).

All That Is Left Is Faith (39:7-11)

What awaits after death? The poet does not know the answer, but he does know "my hope is in thee" (v. 7). He prayed for divine forgiveness before he died (v. 8). Faith and repentance were his way of seeking relief. He felt that his serious illness was punishment for his sin (as in Ps. 38). The problem was that this punishment was consuming him "like a moth" (v. 11) eating clothes.

A Prayer of Desperation (39:12-13)

With beautiful poetry the psalmist prayed for God to hear him. He confessed that he was merely a pilgrim, a "passing guest" on the earth (v.

12). But if God's punishment was not soon lifted, he would pass away completely! (v. 13).

The prayer and psalm end abruptly and not on a note of bright hope. There is no indication that his prayer was heard and answered. While no assurance is given, the one positive note here is the psalmist's enduring faith. How much brighter should be our faith when we have the hope of glory! This psalm should make us appreciate the gospel of our risen Lord even more.

Psalm 40: A Testimony to Answered Prayer

Everyone who has ever experienced answered prayer can identify with the message of this psalm. It contains a dual truth: Amid suffering, believers can know the joy of the Lord's presence (vv. 1-11). Amid joy, there is continuing human need (vv. 13-17).

This truth squares with human experience; sorrow and joy often live on opposite sides of the same street. The psalm was a personal testimony given in public worship.

Many commentators think we have two psalms here. The first part of the psalm is a thanksgiving, and the second is a lament. The two are connected by a transitional verse—12. The second half of the psalm (vv. 13-17) is repeated as Psalm 70.

A Testimony to Answered Prayer (40:1-12)

The psalmist "waited patiently" for the Lord, not with defeated resignation but in expectant hope. It appears that there was no immediate answer, but God did eventually come to the psalmist's rescue. He "heard my cry" (v. 1).

The Lord drew the poet up from the Pit or Sheol. He was sinking down into the miry clay of death, like a man helpless in quicksand. Note the contrast: the Lord lifted him up. He "set my feet upon a rock," making him secure (v. 2). The rock is God himself (Ps. 31:2).

The results of the psalmist's deliverance were twofold: God gave him "a new song" of praise—singing we go! Many would see what God did for him and put their trust in the Lord (v. 3). Who can measure the influence of a good example?

The beatitude in verse 4 is much like Psalm 1:1-3. Happy is the person who trusts in the Lord. He does not go astray after false gods (literally "lies").

The poet celebrated God's mighty acts on his behalf (v. 5). He concluded that they were incomparable and innumerable. Counting your blessings can be a helpful spiritual exercise.

The psalmist expressed his gratitude by giving himself to the Lord in self-dedication. He knew the Lord would rather have his obedience than a thank offering. God delights more in an ethical life-style than in ritual correctness. This was the message of the great prophets (Amos 4:4-5; Hos. 6:6; Jer. 7:22-23). "I delight to do thy will . . . thy law is within my heart" (v. 8). He told the good news of his deliverance, giving his testimony to the congregation (v. 9).

In verse 10 we have a listing of the attributes of the Lord: saving power, faithfulness, and steadfast love. God is altogether trustworthy. It was this which called forth the poet's praise.

The psalm makes a transition from thanksgiving to lament at verse 12. The poet was suffering from serious illness and distress. He could not see his way out of his problem. He felt overwhelmed by evil and trouble.

A Prayer for Future Deliverance (40:13-17)

The psalmist cried out for deliverance (v. 13) from his enemies (v. 14). Their mockery caused him to pray for their punishment (v. 15). He felt his own weakness (v. 17) but was equally aware of God's power: "Great is the Lord!" (v. 16). Therefore, he could trust God to take care of him.

See Psalm 70 for a repetition of this part of the psalm. The blending of two poems in Psalm 40 is appropriate, for joy and suffering are often two sides of the same coin. They may both be experienced "cheek by jowl."

Psalm 41: Blessed Are the Merciful

Psalm 1 celebrated the happiness of a righteous person. Psalm 32 celebrated the blessedness of a forgiven sinner. And Psalm 41 celebrates the happiness of the compassionate. Its first three verses are very similar to Jesus' Beatitude in which he taught that those who show mercy also receive it (Matt. 5:7).

The psalm goes on to express the gratitude of a man who was healed from what appeared to be a terminal illness. Thus he was vindicated before his gleeful enemies, who awaited his death (v. 5).

The Rewards of the Compassionate (41:1-3)

"Blessed is he who considers the poor!" (v. 1). Recall James 1:27.

• The Lord delivers him, protects him, keeps him alive, and sustains him.

• He is called happy or blessed throughout the land.

• His enemies do not get the best of him.

• The Lord heals him from all his sickness. This section sounds a beautifully positive note.

A Lament Against Friend and Enemy (41:4-10)

The psalmist recounted his past distress. He had prayed for healing, acknowledging his sins against God (v. 4). His enemies were malicious. They anxiously awaited his death, like so many vultures (v. 5).

One of the poet's enemies came to visit him. What appeared to be an act of mercy was actually an effort to see how ill he really was and report it to everyone else (v. 6). His enemies started a whisper campaign against him. They speculated as to what terrible sin on his part had brought on this serious sickness. They "imagine the worst" (v. 7). How true to human nature!

Finally, the psalmist's enemies concluded that he had "a deadly thing"—some terminal disease or perhaps a curse. They were convinced that he would never recover (v. 8).

The cruelest blow of all occurred when the poet's best friend joined the ranks of his enemies. The two had shared mutual trust and common meals together, but this "bosom friend" turned against him (v. 9). Jesus quoted the last half of this verse, referring to the treachery of Judas's betrayal (John 13:18).

In verse 10 we have a strange prayer. The poet asked God to be gracious and heal him in order that he might pay his enemies back! His healing would prove them wrong. Jesus taught that we should not try to take revenge on our enemies. Vengeance belongs to God alone (Rom. 12:19). The prayer is, of course, pre-Christian, but it is also very human. It is out of keeping with the psalmist's own attitude in verses 1-3. That, too, shows his humanity (and ours).

Healing Proves to Be Vindication (41:11-12)

God's healing the psalmist fully showed that God was pleased with his integrity. It stopped the tongues of his enemies and showed that his relationship with God, broken by his sin (v. 4), had been restored.

Verse 13 is a benediction to Book I of the Psalms. It is concluded with a double Amen to be repeated by the congregation in worship.

Psalms 42—43: Homesick for God

While these two psalms are separate, they make up a single poem. The poet was a person of deep faith who was living in exile at the headwaters of the Jordan River near snowcapped Mount Hermon, north of the Holy Land. While he could pray to the Lord, he sincerely missed the opportunities for worship at the Temple in Jerusalem. We need the closet of private prayer (Matt. 6:6), but we also need to experience the presence of God in corporate worship (Acts 2:1-4).

The two psalms taken together have three sections, each of which concludes with a refrain (42:5,11; 43:5). The poet gave vivid expression to his longing for God and the experience of public worship.

Thirst for God (42:1-5)

As the deer thirsts for flowing streams in times of drought, so the psalmist longed for the living God, who never fails to satisfy (vv. 1-2). Overwhelmed by his depression and surrounded by scoffers, he thirsted for the comfort of God's presence. As the stream quenches the deer's thirst, so God's steadfast love brought joy and praise to the psalmist's lips (Rev. 21:6; 22:17).

The poet was so homesick for God that he lost all appetite—tears were his only food. Scoffers taunted him, asking, "Where is your God?" (v. 3). Recall the sarcasm hurled at Jesus on the cross (Matt. 27:43). He could have called ten thousand angels.

The psalmist recalled happier days when he had been in the pilgrim's procession going up to the house of God for worship. Those were times of joy and thanksgiving—festive occasions (v. 4).

The refrain occurs first in 42:5. The psalmist talked with himself in an effort to find encouragement and overcome depression. He called on himself to hope and wait for God.

Feeling Overwhelmed (42:6-11)

The author found himself in the north, away from Jerusalem. The sound of the waterfalls or cataracts was like thunder. He thought of the depths of the sea and felt overwhelmed by his depression (v. 7). In the dark night of his soul, the Lord gave him a night song (v. 8). God was still his rock—his source of strength and security. Even so, he felt deserted at times (v. 9). His enemies were still taunting his faith (vv. 3,10). The refrain occurs a second time (v. 11).

Praying for Vindication (43:1-5)

The psalmist asked God to defend him and deliver him from the ungodly (v. 1). The silence and absence of God were at times unbearable (v. 2).

He prayed for God to send his light and truth, benevolent messengers, who would bring him to the "altar of God" again with great joy (v. 4).

This time the refrain emphasized hope and became a shout of triumph (v. 5)! May we all thirst for a vital relationship with God and meaningful worship of God.

Psalm 44: Where on Earth Is God?

What happens to faith in a time of national military defeat? Israel had trusted in God, yet they met with disaster. Their armies were defeated; their citizens were sold into slavery; their cities were razed. The national disgrace and shame were unbearable. Their faith and the facts did not square with each other.

The context in which the psalm was used in worship may be reflected in 2 Chronicles 20:1-19. The king would have read it in a time of national crisis or calamity.

God's Help in Times Past (44:1-3)

The psalmist knew his history and set the present trouble in perspective. Their fathers had related God's mighty acts on behalf of his people in earlier times. The book of Joshua records the events cited here. He drove the Canaanites out and established Israel in the land. Neither their swords nor their might won the victories; God did it on behalf of his people.

Israel's Present Trust in God (44:4-8)

They still acknowledged God as their king, giving him the glory for their triumphs. "In God we trust" could have been their motto. Their faith was not simply in their arms. Because of God's blessings in the past, Israel was confident they could trust him for the present and the future. Then came the bombshell!

When Faith and Fact Do Not Agree (44:9-22)

Despite Israel's faith, they were defeated. God had not marched with their armies, giving victory (v. 9). Some Israelites were slaughtered like sheep, and others were sold into slavery for a pittance (vv. 11-12).

The hardest pill to swallow was the ridicule and scorn of their enemies. The nation was a laughingstock held up to derision (vv. 13-16). Recall the Southern states' condition during the Reconstruction period following the American Civil War.

All this had happened to the Israelites even though they had been faithful to God (vv. 17-18). Their cities were left desolate, inhabited only by jackals (v. 19).

Note the lament in verse 22. Paul quoted it in Romans 8:36 to show that believers often face persecution and death for their faith.

Israel's theological problem was that they believed God blessed in proportion to their obedience and cursed in proportion to their disobedience. Contrast that view with the experience of Job and Isaiah 53.

They Cry for Help (44:23-26)

The poet wondered where God was and concluded that God must be asleep. He prayed to awaken him! This sounds strange to modern Christians. (See Ps. 121:4.) The love of God revealed in Christ was veiled to the psalmist; still, he trusted in God (v. 26).

Routley concludes, "It is well to remember the Dunkirks or Corregidors of national history even in times of tranquillity."[1] Who knows when a comparable faith will be needed again?

Note

1. Erik Routley, *Exploring the Psalms* (Philadelphia: Westminster Press, 1979), p. 68.

Psalm 45: A Royal Wedding

This psalm celebrates a royal wedding. It is a joyous tribute to the king and his bride on a festive occasion. A royal wedding was an event of national importance. It would ensure the continuation of the dynasty (v. 16). The poem is different from any other of the Psalms.

It is not possible to identify the original occasion of the psalm's use. Some have suggested that it may commemorate the marriage of King Ahab to Jezebel. Jerusalem is not mentioned in the psalm. Ahab was from Samaria in the Northern Kingdom, and Jezebel was from Sidon, a

city near Tyre (v. 12). However, since they were a wicked pair, it is unlikely that their wedding poem would have been included in the Psalter.

Later Jewish interpretation applied this royal psalm to the king as the
Messiah and the bride as Israel. Note how the New Testament writer
made use of this concept in Hebrews 1:8-9. The church is considered the
bride of Christ.

To the King (45:1-9)

The poet was excited about his subject. His tongue was as ready as the
pen of a fast stenographer (v. 1). His praise of the king and his bride is
filled with extravagant superlatives. He declared that the king is hand-
some and that his words are winsome. The king also enjoys the blessings
of God (v. 2).

Next, the poet celebrated the king's prowess as a warrior (vv. 3-5). He
wields a mighty sword, rides forth in victory, defends truth and the right,
and fires sharp arrows, putting dread into his foes.

The king will be an ethical ruler, loving justice and hating wrong.
(This section sounds a bit like King Arthur in *Camelot* or Don Quixote de
La Mancha.) The promise in verse 6 is that his divinely established
throne will last forever (a common but vain promise if applied to anyone
less than the Messiah). The king represented God as his adopted son (see
Ps. 2:7).

The king's wedding day was a time of great joy. God himself anoints
the king with "the oil of gladness" (see Ps. 23:5). The king's regal robes
are perfumed; music gladdens the occasion. Pomp is evident in the ivory-
inlaid palace and the gold-bedecked queen (vv. 8-9).

To the New Queen (45:10-15)

Addressing the bride, the poet cited an ingredient in any successful
marriage—leaving one's parents in order to cleave to one's mate (v. 10).
Her allegiance is now to belong to the king, her husband (v. 11). Neighboring states and wealthy families will bestow gifts on the new queen (v.
12).

Next, the poet described the wedding procession. The beautifully
dressed bride leads her attendants into the palace of the king "with joy
and gladness" (v. 15). A splendid scene is depicted here.

The Promise of a Bright Future (45:16-17)

The poet anticipated the birth of sons to the royal couple. He predicted that they would be worthy princes, bringing honor to their father and the praise of the populace.

This celebrative poem shows clearly that the nation was dependent on God. (So is ours.) God blesses the king (v. 2), establishes his throne (v. 6), chooses the king (v. 7), and gives him sons to ensure the future of the kingdom (v. 16).

Psalm 46: The City of God

Here is one of the most influential psalms in the history of the church. It is a hymn in praise of the presence of God. There are two stanzas with a refrain: "The Lord of hosts is with us; the God of Jacob is our refuge" (vv. 7,11). Although the psalm never uses the word *faith*, its theme is faith in the sovereign power and ultimate victory of God.

God, Our Refuge (46:1-3)

These verses refer to God's activity in nature—his creation. They constitute a backward glance. At creation God brought order out of chaos. He continues to exert control over nature. These are crashing sentences, illuminated with flashes of lightning. Recall Jesus' stilling the storm on the Sea of Galilee, saying, "Peace! Be still!" (Mark 4:39).

The teaching of this passage is that though the world about us is disturbed, the faithful need not be frightened. Faith survives because God is our help and refuge. We need have no ultimate fear—not even nuclear holocaust. (See 2 Pet. 3:8-12.) Believers are secure. Faith remains, as God remains, when all else fails (Rom. 8:31-39).

God, Our Help (46:4-7)

He is not only our Creator but also our Sustainer. These verses have a present reference. The city of God was Jerusalem, which had no river like other capitals. Babylon was built on the Euphrates, Egypt alongside the Nile, and Rome on the Tiber. The stream which refreshed Jerusalem was the presence of the living God. (See Rev. 21:1-5a; 22:1-5 for a description of the new Jerusalem.)

As Rome was falling, Augustine looked beyond all earthly cities to the "city of God." Western civilization was headed into the eclipse of the Dark Ages. Yet the church, which was divinely established, would survive. The city of God remains when all earthly cities are destroyed. Note the refrain (v. 7).

God, Our Hope (46:8-11)

This third stanza of the psalm has a future stance. It looks toward what is yet to be. A time is coming when wars will cease and the peace of God will reign. God will be exalted: "Be still, and know that I am God." Here we have a call to quiet trust, as in John Greenleaf Whittier's poem set to a familiar hymn tune:

> Drop thy still dews of quietness,
>   Till all our strivings cease;
> Take from our souls the strain and stress,
>   And let our ordered lives confess
> The beauty of thy peace.

God has all power, and his divine purpose cannot suffer ultimate defeat. He will have the last word. His kingdom will come. His will shall be done on earth as it is in heaven. What a source of encouragement!

Note the refrain again (v. 11). "The Lord of hosts" is a reference to his heavenly armies, the angels. The phrase reminds us of his unseen might which fights evil on our behalf.

"The God of Jacob" is an historical reference. Our faith is not simply "other worldly." It is anchored in history here on earth. God has acted on our behalf. His intervention reveals his will for us. Consider such events as his choice of Abraham, the deliverance of the Israelites in the Exodus, and the sending of his Son, Jesus Christ. Our faith has to do with both here and hereafter. One day the kingdoms of this world shall become the kingdom of our Lord and of his Christ. We express that faith every time we pray the Lord's Prayer.

Psalm 46 also inspired Martin Luther's great Reformation hymn, "A Mighty Fortress Is Our God."

Psalm 47: King of All the Earth

All the festivity and excitement of a coronation is reflected in this psalm—and the king is God himself! The theme of the psalm is found in verse 7: "God is the king of all the earth." Note the ingredients of a coronation included here: the people shout and clap their hands in celebration (v. 1); there is a trumpet fanfare (v. 5); neighboring kings pay their respects; and shields symbolize the king's protection (v. 9). There is also a procession up to the Temple (v. 5).

Scholars have suggested that this is one of six "enthronement psalms" used in Jewish worship on New Year's Day to celebrate God as king of creation and history. (See also Pss. 93; 96—99.) The most striking characteristic of this psalm is its universalism. That is, while God is king of Israel, he is also king of "all peoples" (v. 1).

New Testament parallels to this psalm are found in the Lord's Prayer ("Thy kingdom come") and Revelation 11:15 ("The kingdom of the world has become the kingdom of our Lord and of his Christ, and he shall reign forever and ever").

God Is King of Israel (47:1-5)

"Jacob" in verse 4 stands for the Hebrew nation as well as for their ancestor. Clapping, shouting, and playing of trumpets were parts of the coronation ceremony.

To call God "terrible" (v. 2) means he is to be respected and revered. He defeated the people of Canaan, giving the land to the Jews. Verse 5 describes the triumphant procession going up to the Temple, where God's presence was represented by the ark of the covenant in the holy of holies.

God Is King of All People (47:6-9)

In the jubilant celebration the poet called for singing praise to God four times. Verses 7-8 appear to be either a choral or a congregational response, "For God is the king of all the earth . . . God reigns over the nations; God sits on his holy throne."

"The people of the God of Abraham" in verse 9 refers to his descendants through whom "all the families of the earth shall be blessed" (Gen. 12:3, alternate translation).

God's universal kingship over all the nations of the world is declared four times in this short psalm (vv. 2,7-9). The shields in verse 9 are symbols of God's protection, his providential care.

The poet's vision of God is truly worldwide. He envisioned the ultimate universal reign of the Creator—the kingdom of God. The church lives in anticipation of that time when Jesus will in fact be Lord of all.

Psalm 48: "The City of Our God"

The theme of this psalm is an elaboration of Psalm 46:5—God's presence in Jerusalem. His presence was the city's security. The ancient

Hebrews thought their Holy City could not fall. But in 587 BC it did. This psalm may have been sung by pilgrim worshipers marching through Jerusalem.

The City of the Great King (48:1-3)

The poet began with a declaration, "Great is the Lord." This fact constitutes a call to praise. He called Jerusalem with its Temple on Mount Zion "the city of our God . . . the city of the great King" (God). God himself was Jerusalem's "sure defense" (v. 3), her fortress.

The City Intimidates Its Enemies (48:4-8)

Attacking kings approached Jerusalem. But as soon as they saw this city defended by God "they were astounded." Trembling, they fled in panic and gasped with anguish like a woman in childbirth (v. 6). They were broken up and demolished like mighty merchant ships from Spain in the grip of a storm from the east (v. 7). God had both established and defended Jerusalem in the past. They were confident of his protection in the future.

Touring the City with Praise and Joy (48:9-14)

Pilgrims were invited to tour Jerusalem, taking note of its towers, ramparts, and citadels (vv. 12-13). They were admonished to tell unborn generations that God is the city's God and sure defense "for ever and ever" (v. 14).

The Jew's reverence for the Holy City was similar to that which Christians give to Christ.

Psalm 49: What Money Cannot Buy

The inadequacy of riches and the inevitability of death is the double theme of this wisdom psalm. (Pss. 1 and 37 are also of this type.) It is not a hymn or a prayer addressed to God. It is a proverb from a wise man addressed to people.

Now Hear This (49:1-4)

The wise man's introduction was universal in its appeal. It captured the attention of rich and poor alike. The wise man's proverb promised to solve a riddle (a tough problem) which was of interest to all mankind.

The theme of this psalm was later expanded in the teachings of Jesus in his parables of the rich fool (Luke 12:16-21) and Lazarus and the rich man (Luke 16:19-31). It was exemplified in the text from Jesus, "A man's life does not consist in the abundance of his possessions" (Luke 12:15). The psalm is a warning about the limitations of wealth.

What Money Cannot Buy (49:5-12)

Woe to those who trust in their wealth and boast about their riches. Money cannot postpone death or buy immortality (vv. 7,9). Death is impartial. It takes the wise and the stupid, the wealthy and the poor alike. Those who own vast lands ultimately occupy no more than a grave space (v. 11).

The psalm's refrain is found in verses 12 and 20. Despite all man's pride and pomp, his lot is the same as that of the animals—to die. It is a chilling refrain which points up the stark reality of death.

Death Is Their Shepherd (49:13-14)

The poet continued his theme. The rich were so pleased with themselves. Perhaps they considered themselves self-made men. With biting irony the writer reminded them that death is their shepherd and the grave will be their sheepfold. Sheol (the Pit) will be their home.

A Glimpse of Glory (49:15)

This verse shines like a diamond on black velvet! The dark background of the psalm makes it all the brighter. Old Testament men had no clear view of life after death. Job longed for it (19:25-27) but with no certain revelation of its reality. The psalmist was confident that God would one day do for him what riches could not—ransom his soul from death. "No man can ransom himself" (v. 7). Jesus gave his life as "a ransom for many" (Mark 10:45).

You Cannot Take It with You (49:16-20)

Having sounded this high hope, the psalmist returned to his theme. There is no need to envy or fear the rich (v. 16). When they die they have no pockets in their shrouds. ("How much did he leave?" "Everything!") No matter how happy we are here, death awaits us all (vv. 18-19). The refrain occurs a second time (v. 20).

Put your trust in God, and use your money. Don't reverse the order. This psalm is relevant to our affluent times.

Psalm 50: The Lord, Our Judge

Here is high drama. God summons the world to judgment, both his Chosen People, Israel, and the wicked, He is both plaintiff and judge in the case (compare Isa. 41;43).

This psalm rebukes our "playing church" and calls for heartfelt worship. It is much like the message of the eighth century BC Hebrew prophets.

The Judge of All the Earth (50:1-6)

"The Mighty One," the Creator, summons all the earth "from the rising of the sun to its setting" before the bar of judgment (v. 1). He sits in judgment "out of Zion," Jerusalem. His appearance is similar to that at Mount Sinai (Ex. 19). "Our God comes" in a storm, laced with lightning (v. 3). He calls on heaven and earth to witness the trial of his saints— "my faithful ones" (v. 5). Hear ye, hear ye, "God himself is judge" (v. 6).

The Gift Without the Giver (50:7-15)

God was not displeased that his people brought their sacrifices to him. But they misunderstood the meaning behind their gifts. They assumed that God needed their sacrifice. "Do I eat the flesh of bulls, or drink the blood of goats?" (v. 13). Everything belongs to God, "the cattle on a thousand hills" (v. 10). The motive behind our worship is not God's need—but ours! Therefore, the sacrifice God really wants is our heartfelt worship and thanksgiving (v. 14) and our fellowship with him in prayer (v. 15).

God's ownership of all is the basis of stewardship. He doesn't need our money, but we need to learn the joy of giving. It is a cure for our selfishness.

Testimony Against the Hypocrites (50:16-21)

The wicked could recite the Ten Commandments by heart; yet they were not ethical in their daily lives (v. 16). They despised discipline (v. 17), associated with thieves and adulterers, and slandered their own brothers (vv. 18-20). This passage is similar to Hosea 4:12 and Romans 2:17-24. Their religion was merely an external tradition—not a matter of the heart. Therefore, they must answer to God.

Warning and Promise (50:22-23)

To our peril, we sometimes forget God. When we worship him with thanksgiving, God is honored. When we live ethically and in gratitude for divine grace, we show the fruits of salvation.

It is easier to recite the Ten Commandments than to live by them. It is easier to give our money than to give ourselves. Superficial religion is a constant temptation (Matt. 7:21). God requires our total commitment and obedience to his will. The message of this psalm is quite relevant today.

Psalm 51: A Plea for Pardon

Erik Routley called the psalms "a mirror of life."[1] What an apt description of this penitential psalm. Its setting is the visit of the prophet Nathan to King David and the king's repentance (2 Sam. 12:1-23). The poem reflects the seriousness of sin, the pain of guilt, and the joy of repentance and restoration. A saint is a sinner who has repented. Psalm 51 is a king's confession, which can apply to everyone.

A Plea for Pardon (51:1-2)

We tend to make light of sin, inventing new labels for old evils, such as "the new morality." The Bible is realistic. It describes sin as it is, with the most vivid terms. Three specific words for sin are used in these verses:

Iniquity is a powerful word which means perverse and crooked. It describes fallen human nature, people apart from God.

Transgressions are actions known to be in defiance of what is right. The word means deliberate rebellion (recall Absalom).

Sin literally means "missing the mark" or moral failure. God takes our sin seriously—witness the cross.

The poet also used three words to describe divine forgiveness. "Blot out" means to erase or remove from the record (Isa. 43:25).

"Wash me," he prayed. Forgiveness makes a difference in our soiled lives (Ex. 19:10).

"Cleanse me" (from moral pollution) was his third prayer. Sin leaves us with a bad record and dirty, contaminated lives. Divine forgiveness corrects all this.

A Confession of Sin (51:3-4)

The psalmist was haunted by his guilt (recall Lady Macbeth). The poet acknowledged personal responsibility for his sin. He spoke of "my iniquity . . . my sin . . . my transgressions." There was no blaming others here.

The poet also acknowledged that his sin was against God. He had sinned against Bathsheba, Uriah, the nation, and himself. But most of all, his sin violated God's moral law. When we sin, we break both God's law and God's heart. He suffers due to our sin. Jesus was our suffering Redeemer.

The Context of Sin (51:5)

When the poet spoke of being conceived in sin, he was not casting aspersions on his parents. He was simply saying that he was born into a sinful society of which he became a part. There is collective as well as individual sin and guilt (Isa. 6:5).

To say mankind is "totally depraved" does not mean we are incapable of any good. It means we are never immune from temptation and sin.

A Prayer for Forgiveness (51:6-12)

Notice the vivid way in which the poet prayed:

"Purge me" literally means "unsin." When God forgives us, it is as though we had never sinned, from his point of view.

"Restore the joy" as a prodigal reconciled to his Father.

"Create in me a clean heart, O God." Only God can create, and only God can completely forgive the sinner.

A Promise to Share (51:13-19)

The psalmist promised to teach sinful people the ways of God. He asked only that God deliver him from his sin. His petition also calls upon God to open his mouth in order that he might praise God to others. The sincerity of the psalmist is seen in his giving God the sacrifice of "a broken and contrite heart" (v. 17). God always accepts repentance.

Note

1. Erik Routley, *Exploring the Psalms* (Philadelphia: Westminster Press, 1975), p. 11.

Psalm 52: The Boastful Wicked

The psalmist accused the wicked braggart of trusting in riches instead of the Lord (vv. 1-4,7). Then he predicted their downfall (vv. 5-7). Finally, he announced the security of those who trust in God's steadfast love (vv. 8-9). The title of this psalm refers to the account in 1 Samuel 22.

The Braggart (52:1-7)

The psalmist asked why the "big man" brags about his wickedness (v. 1). He was guilty of the sins of a sharp tongue, delighting in lies and destructive words (vv. 2-4). Remember the childish taunt, "Words can't hurt me." Adults know better.

A prediction of peril is announced. The ungodly will be broken down and uprooted (v. 5). They will become a laughingstock because they made riches their refuge and not God (vv. 6-7).

The Godly (52:8-9)

The psalmist and others who trust in the Lord are blessed. They will flourish like an olive tree planted near the Temple (v. 8). The righteous trust in God's unfailing love, express their thanksgiving, and share their faith (v. 9).

The psalm teaches that our boast is to be in the Lord and not in our possessions (see 1 Cor. 1:21).

Psalm 53: Human Depravity

See the commentary on Psalm 14. These appear to be two versions of the same psalm describing the sinfulness of mankind.

Psalm 54: "Save Me, O God"

This prayer for deliverance is both a cry for help and a confession of the psalmist's confidence in God. The background referred to in the title is found in 1 Samuel 23:15-21.

A Prayer for Rescue (54:1-3)

Note the parallelism in verse 1: "Save me . . . vindicate me" and "by thy name . . . by thy might." Ruthless men threatened the life of the psalmist (v. 3). He prayed to be saved from them.

Anticipation of Deliverance (54:4-7)

The psalmist was confident that God would help him (v. 4). His enemies would be punished, and he would be vindicated. Out of gratitude he anticipated bringing "a freewill offering" to the Lord (v. 6). It was not a required offering but a spontaneous expression of his thanksgiving.

The principal characteristic of the psalms of lamentation is the constant faith they portray. The poets always believed that God would hear their prayer in his own time and act to save them. These psalms grew out of felt need and always addressed God with confident trust.

Psalm 54 is often read on Good Friday. God vindicated Jesus by the resurrection, showing that the charges of his enemies were false.

Psalm 55: On the Wings of a Dove

This harsh lament is also a moving personal prayer. It begins with a fourfold petition that God will "give ear" to his prayer, "hide not" from the psalmist but "attend to" his request and "answer" him (vv. 1-2). The psalm is highly charged with emotion, though the specifics of his trouble are not told. This gives the poem universal appeal to all who face serious problems. Note how the psalmist tried to deal with his difficulties.

He Longed to Escape (55:1-8)

Many bear awful burdens and limiting handicaps. This psalm reflects a crescendo of distress. One reaction is the desire to escape, to get away from it all. "O that I had wings like a dove! I would fly away and be at rest . . . I would lodge in the wilderness" (vv. 6-7). There he might be safe from the storm of trouble (v. 8). The fantasy of escape may serve as an emotional safety valve, but it is not the answer to our deepest need in times of trouble.

Some escape into dreams or a flight into the past, "the good old days." Others escape an unpleasant present by living only for the future. Some escape into their work and others into illness, or drink, or even suicide. Flight from trouble was the psalmist's first reaction.

He Lashed Out (55:9-15,20-21,23)

Next the poet turned on his enemies with a vengeance. He fought back, struck out. His initial desire for flight now turned to fight. The poet was afflicted by his enemies, and he cursed them (vv. 9-11).

However, the hardest thing the psalmist faced was the betrayal of his friend (vv. 13-14, 20-21). The two of them had been close, sharing precious conversation and even worship of God (v. 14). All the while his friend's words had been "smoother than butter," covering the hostility in his heart. Verse 21 is vivid!

The psalmist knew how to deal with his enemies. The betrayal of his friend cut him to the quick. (Recall Judas.) He asked God to reward his enemies for their treachery (vv. 15,23). Confusion of tongues in verse 9 may be a reflection of the experience of the race at the Tower of Babel (Gen. 11:5-9).

He Took His Burden to the Lord (55:16-19,22)

The psalmist turned to God in consistent prayer, "evening and morning and at noon" (v. 17). He was confident of divine deliverance (v. 18).

The climax of the psalm, the poet's ultimate trust in God, is seen in verse 22: "Cast your burden on the Lord, and he will sustain you." God is not our porter, but our companion. He does not always take away our burden, but he gives us grace to bear it. Prayer changes things—both circumstances and the person who prays. Though friends may betray him, he can still trust in God (v. 23b). Our only sure refuge is God.

Psalm 55 was written by a soul in great anguish. He was troubled and betrayed. His reactions were true to life. We act much the same. The great lesson here is that we can trust in God when all else fails us. It is important to distinguish between problems, which we can solve, and life circumstances, which we cannot.

Psalm 56: Trust in God

Here we have a mixture of lament over the psalmist's enemies and the confession of his faith in God.

Appeal for Gracious Help (56:1-7)

The psalmist was oppressed, trampled by his enemies. In such peril he realized he was beyond mere human help (v. 4b). In a memorable text he declared his faith, "When I am afraid, I put my trust in thee" (v. 3).

The poet's enemies were lurking and ruthless—out to get him (vv. 5-6). He asked that God would repay them for their crimes (v. 7).

Heaven Knows What We Suffer (56:8-13)

It is a comfort to know that God is aware of the burdens we bear. Here the poet painted a lovely picture of God's awareness. God keeps count of the psalmist's sleepless nights. He even saves the poet's tears in a bottle! (v. 8).

No wonder he confessed his faith, "God is for me" (v. 9). Therefore, he trusted in the Lord (v. 11), praised him (v. 10), and brought his "thank offerings" (v. 12). It was the Lord who kept him safe and delivered him from danger (v. 13). We have a convincing confession of faith in this psalm.

Psalm 57: In the Lion's Den

This psalm has twin themes: a plea for help and a prayer of praise. The two are tied together by the poet's confession of his faith.

The Psalmist's Trust (57:1-3)

He began with a cry for God's mercy and help. "Without faith it is impossible to please him [God]" (Heb. 11:6). The poet knew he would be secure "in the shadow of thy wings" (v. 1). Despite his peril, he felt safe "till the storm passes by."

The psalmist had faith to believe God would "send from heaven" and save him (v. 3). When we are at our wit's end, having exhausted all human resources, we look for help from beyond. Read Romans 8:28.

Psalmist in the Lion's Den (57:4-6)

Like Daniel (6:16-24), the psalmist found himself in the midst of man-eating lions. They were his enemies. They were powerfully armed with spears and arrows for teeth and tongues like sharp swords. Those fierce enemies could cut his reputation to pieces. He was prey to their slander and false accusations.

They were also cunning hunters, setting a snare and digging a pit for him—only to fall into it themselves (v. 6). Christians face an enemy, too—satanic power (1 Pet. 5:8). It pays to be on guard.

The Psalmist's Faith in the Midst of Fear (57:7-11)

Note the pattern of lament, confession of faith, and praise. It is repeated twice in the psalm. The poet sang of his steadfast faith in verse 7.

He was unshaken despite the danger he faced. He could sing even in the midst of trouble.

The poet called for nature to awake and rejoice with him. He even went out to awaken the dawn (it usually awakens us). His joy was so complete that he could not wait for daylight to share it—like a proud father whose child has been born during the night. His thanksgiving was too good to keep to himself (v. 9).

The faithfulness and love of God called forth his praise. He exalted the Lord and ascribed glory to him "over all the earth!" (v. 11).

Here we have an example of faith overcoming fear. The setting indicated in the title of the psalm was David's flight for his life from King Saul (1 Sam. 24:4). This hymn of deliverance is used as an Easter psalm (note vv. 3-5).

The psalmist's faith is self-evident. John Durham concludes, "If such faith does not move mountains, it is at any rate not daunted by them."[1]

Note

1. John Durham, "Psalms," *The Broadman Bible Commentary* (Nashville: Broadman Press, 1971), Vol. 4, p. 287.

Psalm 58: Judge of People and Angels

Despite all signs to the contrary, "there is a God who judges on earth" (v. 11). Thus, the theme of this psalm is stated with great assurance.

God judges both wicked heavenly beings and wicked human beings. The word "gods" in verse 1 is translated "rulers" in *The New English Bible*. It can refer to unjust angels who fail to do the Creator's will. Or it may be a sarcastic way of referring to "lordly" human rulers who abuse their power. In either case they must answer to God who judges all.

A Call for Justice (58:1-2)

Those who are supposed to judge fairly "devise wrongs" and "deal out violence on earth." What hope has a man when the judge is crooked? They, too, must stand under the judgment of another.

Wicked Persons (58:3-5)

It appeared to the psalmist that they were bent on evil from their birth (v. 3). This speaks to the reality of human depravity. It is not that they are incapable of doing right. Rather, they choose to do what is wrong.

The poet said they are like deaf snakes who cannot be controlled by the snake charmer's spell. Their venom is slander and lies.

A Sevenfold Curse (58:6-9)

The number seven in Scripture stands for perfection or completeness. The psalmist pronounced a sevenfold curse on the wicked: May God break their teeth and pull their fangs. May they evaporate like water and wither like trampled grass. May they dissolve like a crawling slug leaving a trail of slime. May they be stillborn as a result of spontaneous abortion. May they be like dry thornbushes consumed in the fire. How vivid! The poet showed a great deal of imagination.

The Righteous Rejoice (58:10-11)

God brings vengeance upon the wicked to the delight of the righteous. Verse 10 paints a gory scene. The point is that all the world will one day meet its Judge and justice will prevail.

Psalm 59: Prayer for Deliverance

Here is a lament against the poet's and the nation's enemies. They are characterized as a pack of howling dogs (vv. 6,14). In verses 9,17 we have the refrain which divides the psalm into two sections. *The New English Bible* translation has the poem open (v. 1) and close (v. 17) referring to God as "my strong tower." He is the believer's citadel or defense tower.

A Plea for Deliverance (59:1-9)

The psalmist prayed for divine deliverance, asserting his own innocence (v. 3*b*). He asked to be protected from his vicious enemies. He invited God to look at that lurking bunch of dogs (v. 3*a*). Then he called on the Almighty to "rouse" himself to punish them (vv. 4-5). His enemies are graphically portrayed as a pack of wild dogs: howling, prowling, and snarling against him (vv. 6-7). They think they are so powerful, but they amuse the Almighty. He laughs at them (v. 8). The refrain occurs in verse 9. God is the poet's fortress.

A Prayer for Help (59:10-17)

In verse 11 the psalmist asked that God not slay his enemies. Let them remain as a lesson to the righteous. But then his sense of outraged justice flared into a prayer for their destruction (v. 13).

Note the reappearance of verse 6 in verse 14: "Each evening they come back, howling like dogs and prowling about the city."

In contrast to his enemies, the confident psalmist sang in praise of God's power and protection (vv. 16-17). God's love was his fortress and refuge. We can always depend on the Lord.

Psalm 60: A Nation's Prayer

Israel had suffered a military defeat and felt rejected by God. The occasion may be that described in 1 Samuel 8. However, the poem was probably read by the king or some other military leader at other times as well, when God failed to march "with our armies" (v. 10). The oracle found in verses 6-8 is repeated in Psalm 108:7-9. This psalm is similar to Psalm 44.

The King's Complaint (60:1-5)

The nation had experienced defeat in battle. This was taken as a sure sign of God's rejection and anger (v. 1). It was as devastating as an earthquake (v. 2). The people were still tottering from the shock. They were in such disarray that they reeled like drunken men (v. 3). Defeat was the cup of divine wrath.

The banner God raised for them was not a rallying point for counterattack. Rather, it was someplace beyond the range of their enemies' arrows (v. 4). The military leader then prayed for victory (v. 5).

The Oracle of God (60:6-8)

God's anger is formidable (v. 1), but it is not final. He still loved Israel. He promised to restore the nation and subdue their rebellious neighboring lands. God is pictured here as a giant warrior. He will extend his control over countries on both sides of the Jordan River. He will make Ephraim, the most powerful tribe, his helmet. Judah, King David's tribe, will become his scepter (v. 7).

Like a warrior returning from battle, God will wash his hands in the Dead Sea (in the land of Moab) and toss his shoes onto Edom. He will shout victory over the plains of Philistia (in the west). This was an early representation of the kingdom of God or his rule, which was later expanded in the New Testament.

A Prayer for God's Help (60:9-12)

The leader prayed for the safety of a fortress city such as Petra in Edom (v. 9). He asked divine help "for vain is the help of man!" (v. 11). With God's help they could defeat their enemies (v. 12). Thus, the psalm concludes on the glad note of expected victory.

This psalm reinforces the truth of God's sovereign power. He is in control of human destiny—then and now.

Psalm 61: Lead Me to the Rock

This psalm is a prayer that God will lead the poet "to the rock that is higher than I" (v. 2). Caught in a flood of trouble, he looked to the safety of God's presence.

The King's Prayer (61:1-5)

This is taken by some commentators to be a royal prayer. First, we have the king's petition to be heard (v. 1) "from the end of the earth" (v. 2). Some take this to mean the psalmist was in exile. Others think the phrase means he is near death. Most likely the reference is not geographical but spiritual. The poet was "at the end of his rope" and experienced the feeling of God's absence. Thus he prayed that God would lead him to the rock that is higher. This could stand for Mount Moriah on which the Temple was built. But a better interpretation is that the rock is God himself (see Ps. 18:2).

God was the poet's refuge and "strong tower" of security (v. 3). The psalmist prayed that he might dwell forever in the safety of the divine Presence (v. 4). "Tent" stands for the Temple. "The shelter of thy wings" means God's care and protection (see Ps. 17:8).

The mood of the psalm changes to bright assurance at verse 5.

A Prayer for the King (61:6-7)

The congregation or chorus would offer this prayer for the king, who was God's representative. Their petition for his long life was also a prayer that his dynasty might be enduring. This would assure the nation of stability under God's protection. The king was to be watched over by two guardian angels: steadfast love and faithfulness (v. 7).

The Poet's Promise (61:8)

The psalmist's response was one of praise and keeping his promises (vows) to God. Gratitude to God is always a proper response for God's people to make.

Psalm 62: God Alone

In this affirmation of faith the psalmist placed his ultimate trust in God alone. His political enemies were out to destroy him (vv. 3-4). He discovered that his security was in God, "my rock." Note his experience with both God and men.

Trust in God (62:1-2,5-7)

The poet waited "in silence" on the Lord. We are such activists that it is hard for us to wait on anything or anyone. We want instant solutions to our problems. We assume that enough money, enough knowledge, or enough effort can solve anything. That is not always the case.

The psalmist had a more accurate insight. He found God to be his "salvation . . . rock . . . fortress." He looked to God to deliver him and defend his honor (v. 7).

The Psalmist's Enemies (62:3-4)

The poet's foes were out to bring him down. They kept hitting him with unrelenting pressure. They were like men trying to shatter an already tottering stone wall (v. 3).

His enemies were two-faced. With their mouths they praised him, but inwardly they were cursing him (v. 4).

The Psalmist's Advice (62:8-12)

The psalmist counseled his contemporaries to trust in God at all times. They were not to put their trust in extortion, robbery or riches (v. 10). He found that persons don't count for much. Ordinary people are only a puff of wind, and important people are but a delusion. Put both in the balance scale, and they go up "lighter than a breath" (v. 9).

The poet learned from experience to trust God's power and love (vv. 11-12). God will punish the wicked and reward the righteous. Such trust is the way to spiritual serenity.

Psalm 63: Thou Art My God

This is an early psalm which predates the Exile. (Note the mention of the king in v. 11.) The poet had a personal faith relationship with God.

Many emotions are expressed in the psalm: longing (vv. 1-2), praise (vv. 3-5), confidence (vv. 6-8), judgment (vv. 9-10), and prayer (vv. 4,11).

The Psalmist's Faith in God (63:1-8)

He longed for God with his whole being, "soul" and "flesh" (v. 1). He thirsted for God as a man in the parched desert thirsts for water. In worship the poet experienced God's presence, power, and glory (v. 2). He concluded that God's steadfast love is more precious than life, mere biological existence (v. 3). In verse 4 the psalmist practiced both praise and prayer. Having the hands lifted up was the Jewish position of prayer, not kneeling with bowed head.

Experiencing life in the presence of God was like enjoying a rich banquet (v. 5). He felt as though he were feasting on God. The quiet hours of the night became a time for meditation and reflection on the greatness and protection of God (vv. 6-7). Note the psalmist's poetic way of describing his dependence on God: "My soul clings to thee; thy right hand upholds me" (v. 8).

The Psalmist's Enemies (63:9-11)

The poet's enemies were God's enemies and the king's enemies, as well. They will go down to death (v. 9) and be given to the sword; they will not be buried (v. 10). The king will rejoice at their defeat, and he will rejoice in the Lord (v. 11).

The golden text of the psalm is verse 3: "Thy steadfast love is better than life."

Psalm 64: "Nobody Knows"

Here we have a personal lament, "my complaint" (v. 1), against the psalmist's slanderous enemies. They think their plots are such well-kept secrets that no one will ever know. They think they can get away with wrongdoing. Not so, declared the psalmist! God knows what evil they plot, and one day everyone else will know what they are up to. Evil will be found out!

The Poet's Petition (64:1-6)

His enemy is secretive and scheming (vv. 1-2). Note the vivid metaphors in verse 3: they "whet their tongues like swords" and "aim bitter words like arrows." Sharp and stinging speech is shot from ambush by cowardly enemies (v. 4).

The poet's enemies never suspect that their identity will be known. They have been so cunning and secretive that they are sure they can do evil and go undetected. But people are smart. They are not fools. They can figure out what is going on (v. 6).

The Poet's Request Granted (64:7-10)

The psalmist was confident that God would judge his enemies. He was so confident that he could speak of it as though it were already an accomplished fact.

His enemies shot slanderous words from cover. God would send his arrows of lightning at them (v. 7). They would be struck down suddenly.

The result will be that "the righteous rejoice" (v. 10) and "all men will fear" the Lord (v. 9). Evil does not triumph for long.

Psalm 65: God's Bounty

Praise is due God for his spiritual blessing (forgiveness) and for his bountiful provision of the good earth. This is the theme of beautiful Psalm 65. The Davidic hymn was sung in the spring, celebrating the rains which make fertile land productive.

Praise in the Temple (65:1-4)

The courtyards of God's holy Temple ring with hymns and prayers of praise. He has forgiven his people's sins (v. 3). They enjoy his presence in worship (v. 4).

God's Mighty Acts (65:5-8)

God delivers and saves his people (v. 5). By his creative power he raised the mountains and calmed the "roaring . . . seas . . . waves . . . tumult" (vv. 6-7). Morning and evening are sent by God and "shout for joy" (v. 8).

God's Mighty Provision (65:9-13)

"Every perfect gift is from above" (Jas. 1:17). The psalmist would agree. God waters the earth. This vital provision was especially important for those living in arid Israel. The failure of winter rains meant famine. Soft rainfall filled the furrows and made the fertile soil productive.

With a poet's eye he described the rain-washed wilderness dripping with freshness (v. 12). The green meadows were "clothed" with white flocks, and the fertile valleys wore a waving mantle of grain. Small wonder all nature will "shout and sing together for joy" (v. 13).

God chooses people, forgives their sins, and satisfies them with the bounty of the good earth—what a call to praise!

Psalm 66: Gratitude, Corporate and Personal

This is a joyful hymn of praise on behalf of the nation and the psalmist. First, it recites the mighty acts of God toward Israel. Then it recalls how God has answered the prayers of an individual. Its missionary tone is similar to Isaiah 40—66.

The Nation's Praise of God (66:1-12)

This psalm begins with the same words as the Hundredth. In the first stanza all people are invited to praise God: "All the earth worships thee" (vv. 1-4). The second stanza describes God's mighty deliverance in the Exodus (vv. 5-7). The trials of the nation in the Exile are also cited (vv. 10-12).

The poet's description of oppression is vivid—like the hot fire which refines silver (v. 10). The people felt as though they were trapped in a net with no way of escape (v. 11). Others overwhelmed them, and they "went through fire and through water" (v. 12).

Yet God delivered his people from slavery in Egypt and captivity in Babylon.

The Psalmist's Praise of God (66:13-20)

The psalmist paid his vows in gratitude for God's deliverance when he was in trouble (vv. 13-14). Out of gratitude he brought many offerings: rams, bulls, and goats (v. 15). The poet must have been a wealthy man.

The second stanza of this second half of the psalm is an outpouring of gratitude. The poet was sincere (v. 18). God truly answered his prayers, and he in turn blessed the Lord (vv. 17,19-20). Gratitude is essential. Jesus illustrated this truth in his dealing with the grateful leper (Luke 17:11-19). Selected verses from this psalm have traditionally been used in Easter worship.

Psalm 67: A Hymn at Harvest

This harvest hymn (v. 6) begins with the ancient blessing of Aaron (Num. 6:24-26). "God's face shining upon us" is a poetic way of speaking about divine favor. It means "may God be pleased with us." Psalm 65 anticipates the harvest. This psalm is an expression of thanks for it, at the Feast of Tabernacles (Lev. 23:34).

God blessed Isarael (vv. 1-3). But he also judges (rules fairly) and guides the other nations of the earth (vv. 4-5). He is due their praise, as well: "Be glad and sing for joy."

God provides the bountiful harvest. He blesses us, and all people everywhere should revere and worship the Lord (vv. 6-7).

Note the strong missionary thrust of this psalm. Gratitude to God is a motive for Christian missions. The Hebrew faith delivered people from the fear of nature and nature worship (a cruel religion). God is shown to be the Creator of nature. As its Lord, he is in control; and his children need not live in fear.

Psalm 68: God Is King

This is considered the toughest psalm to interpret. It became a battle song of the Protestant Reformation. It is a collection of short hymns used in the dramatic worship of Israel, celebrating God as King. Its roots are found in the Song of Deborah (Judg. 5).

An Invocation (68:1-3)

These words were sung at the beginning of the processional. The ark of the covenant, representing God's presence, would lead the worshipers ("Let God arise"). God's enemies flee before him, but the righteous are joyful.

God's Actions in History (68:4-18)

God is the ideal King who reverses the fortunes of those who are oppressed. Next, we have a rehearsal of God's historic actions on behalf of his people in the Exodus (vv. 7-10). (See also Judg. 5:4-5.) These events include leaving Egypt, wandering in the wilderness, receiving the Law at Mount Sinai, and preparing to enter Canaan.

The defeat of Sisera is a typical example of the victories God gave Israel (vv. 11-14).

God chose Mount Zion for his abode. He came there from Mount Sinai, leading captives and receiving gifts. The imagery is that of a warrior king in triumphal procession. Paul applied this scene to the victorious Christ after his resurrection (v. 18; Eph. 4:8).

God, Our Savior (68:19-23)

God is the source of our salvation (v. 19). The psalmist blessed the Lord for delivering him from death and from his enemies. The "hairy crown" refers to a warrior's oath not to cut his hair until he has defeated his enemy in battle. In verse 23 the poet spoke in no uncertain terms of vengeance.

Worship Processional (68:24-27)

A great procession of worshipers go up to the sanctuary to worship. They are led by singers who are followed by young women, princes, and minstrels. Note how they bless the Lord (v. 26).

God's Majesty and Power (68:28-35)

Various nations were told to acknowledge God's might and majesty. Egypt was one nation singled out. "The beasts that dwell among the reeds" are the crocodiles and hippopotamuses who lived in the marshes along the Nile River. Ethiopia was also asked to recognize the God of Israel who strikes awe in those who worship him (vv. 31,35). All nations were invited to sing his praise.

The worship of God by many nations has become a reality with the spread of the gospel.

Psalm 69: Reproach for Serving God

There is a prophetic character to this psalm. It was frequently quoted in the New Testament with reference to Jesus' ministry and suffering—he was smitten, insulted, and wounded. Seventeen quotations from this psalm appear in the Gospels, Acts, and Romans. The psalmist's plight was much like that of Jeremiah (v. 9). He suffered severely for his devotion to God. The poem is a lamentation.

The Poet's Predicament (69:1-12)

The psalmist cried out for God to save him (v. 1), describing his plight as that of a man caught in a flood or quicksand (vv. 2-5). He grew weary waiting for divine deliverance.

The psalmist's enemies were many and fierce. They hated him without cause and were out to destroy him (v. 4). Like Job, he did not claim to be sinless (v. 5). He had been reproached because of his faith (vv. 7,9). His own brothers did not recognize him (v. 8). Even the town drunks made fun of him (v. 12).

The Psalmist's Prayer (69:13-29)

He asked for God's help and rescue lest "the deep swallow me" (v. 15). He wanted deliverance from his enemies. After all, heaven knew what he suffered (v. 19). It is a comfort to remember that God knows and understands what we face.

The poet received no sympathy or understanding, only scorn and reproach (vv. 20-21).

In the next verses (22-29) the psalmist cursed his enemies eloquently. He asked that they might go blind and be afflicted with palsy. He prayed that the divine anger might be vented on those who hated both him and God. Asking the ultimate punishment, he wanted his foes "blotted out of the book of the living" (v. 28). This is similar to Psalm 22.

While Christians may be offended by the psalmist's curses, at least he was honest with the Lord about how he felt. When we pray, the Lord does not want us to play games. He wants us to be honest. Only after that does assurance come.

The Psalmist's Praise (69:30-36)

He promised to give thanks to the Lord (v. 30). Those who are oppressed will see how the Lord delivers him and "be glad" (v. 32).

Finally, the psalmist called on heaven and earth to praise the Lord (v. 34). God will save Zion and rebuild the cities of Judah (v. 35). This is probably an indication that the psalm was written while the poet was in exile in Babylon.

The psalm has both bright spots and dark ones. So does our pilgrimage.

Psalm 70

This psalm is almost identical with Psalm 40:13-17. See the commentary on Psalm 40.

Psalm 71: An Aged Man's Prayer

We have here a highly personal psalm. Note how many times the poet used the personal pronouns, I, my, me. It is the prayer of an old man in lament, confession, and praise. The psalm is similar to and quotes from others (22;31;35;40;57). Still, it is an authentic composition, not merely a mosaic of bits and pieces taken from the work of others.

The Old Man's Doubt (71:1-21)

The psalmist trusted the Lord despite his distress. God was considered his fortress, refuge, and rock. He had trusted the Lord from his youth (v. 5) and had served him all his life (v. 6b).

The elderly poet's enemies thought that God had forsaken him and that they could take advantage of him with impunity (vv. 11-12). In verses 9 and 18a we have the poignant prayer of the elderly, that God would not forsake him in his old age. He had been a faithful member of the covenant community. If spared, he promised to proclaim God's might to subsequent generations (v. 18b).

The psalmist recalled God's providential care in times past (v. 20). He trusted the Lord to spare him and revive him again (vv. 20b-21).

The Old Man's Praise (71:22-24)

The greatness of God almost overwhelmed him (v. 19). This led him to praise the Lord with the harp and lyre, with his lips and tongue. His enemies have been routed (v. 24b). In verse 22 he addressed God as the "Holy One of Israel." Compare Psalms 78:41; 89:18.

Whatever our age, we may trust and praise God.

Psalm 72: A Prayer for the King

Isaac Watts' hymn "Jesus Shall Reign Where'er the Sun" is based on this psalm. The poem was probably written by someone in the court on behalf of the king. It is a royal psalm and may have been used in conjunction with coronations.

Righteous Rule (72:1-4)

The poet prayed that the king, the royal son, might rule with God's justice and righteousness (vv. 1-2). He also asked for prosperity, a sign of divine favor (v. 3), and for the king to defend the poor and crush their oppressors (v. 4).

Long Life (72:5-7)

He asked that the king might "live while the sun endures." This did not imply his immortality. It was more a prayer for the perpetuation of his dynasty and for his rule to be as welcome and prosperous as the life-giving spring showers. After the first mowing, spring rains produced an even more abundant crop. The same Hebrew word is translated "prosperity" and "peace" in this passage *(shalom).*

Dominion from Sea to Sea (72:8-17)

The poet prayed that the king's rule might extend "from sea to sea" (from the Mediterranean to the Persian Gulf). "The River" was probably the Euphrates. Tarshish was Spain. Sheba was in Arabia and Seba in Ethiopia (Africa). These were the limits of the world known to the psalmist.

He prayed that the king's enemies would "lick the dust!" (v. 9)—bow before him paying homage. The king is to be the champion of the powerless (vv. 12-14). The psalmist hoped that the king, like Abraham, would be the channel of divine blessings to "all nations" (v. 17b).

Signs of God's favor on his rule will include: long life, fruitful harvests, a growing population, and fame which lasts "as long as the sun!" (v. 17a).

Conclusion to Book II (72:18-20)

Here we have a doxology which marks the end of the second division of the Psalter. Verse 20 is an editorial footnote indicating that there are no further psalms of David. How appropriate is the closing prayer:

> Blessed be the Lord. . . .
> Blessed be his glorious name for ever;
>   may his glory fill the whole earth!

Psalm 73: The Conversion of a Skeptic

This psalm is the testimony of a skeptic who became a confirmed believer. It is the story of one man's pilgrimage from doubt to faith, from despair to assurance. We find it true to human experience.

The Theme Is Stated (73:1-3)

Mankind has always been troubled by the problem of evil—why does a good God permit it? Old Testament people had an even more acute problem. They had no clear revelation of life after death. They felt that the righteous were blessed by God and the wicked punished here on earth. The prosperity of the wicked and the suffering of the righteous turned that theology wrong side out and stood it on its head. It nearly caused the psalmist to lose his faith! This was Job's problem, too.

The poet began by stating his theme: "Truly God is good to the upright" and to the "pure in heart" (v. 1). Still, he almost lost his faith when he saw "the prosperity of the wicked" (v. 3). He was jealous of them for a time. This inequity has been a stumbling block for many.

The Darkness of Doubt (73:4-14)

Look at the prosperous wicked! They are proud, violent oppressors. Yet they never appear to suffer pain. They are in perfect health (v. 4) and never in trouble. They are indulgent gluttons (v. 7) while others go hungry. They are irreverent scoffers who don't think God is aware of their meanness (v. 11). Ironically, they are well thought of in the community (v. 10). (Who finds fault with rich men? They must be smart.) Everything they touch turns to gold (v. 12).

What good did it do the psalmist to live the clean life? All he got for it was trouble (vv. 13-14). These circumstances are enough to try anyone's faith. The psalmist's candor here is impressive.

The Brightness of Faith Affirmed (73:15-20)

The psalmist was wearied by trying to figure out the answer to his question (v. 16). The turning point came when he went to worship (v. 17). Suddenly he realized that the wicked were not as secure as they seemed. One false step, and they would fall to ruin (v. 18). Their prosperity—indeed, their lives themselves—were temporary. They could lose it all in a flash (v. 19). They were as insubstantial as a dream (v. 20).

The psalmist repented of his lack of faith and bitterness (vv. 21-22). He realized that he was in fellowship with God, who upheld him, guided him, and would receive him "to glory" (v. 23-24).

The poet did not get an answer to the problem of evil or the prosperity of the wicked any more than Job did. Those questions are unanswerable here on earth. They are bound up in the mystery of a sovereign God. What the psalmist did get was the fulfillment of being in the presence of God. God is "my portion for ever" (v. 26). The reward of faith and the ultimate answer of prayer is "to be near God" (v. 28). Here we have a contrast between the passing pleasures of the sinner and the enduring peace of those who are friends of God.

Human nature seems to cause us to ask unanswerable questions and seek rational explanations of everything we do not understand. Recall a child's innumerable questions. But the truth is that life *is* often unfair. We are fallen sinners who live in an imperfect world. While we may never have all the answers to our questions, we do have God. We can trust him, for he is our Father. "God is good" (v. 1).

The golden text of this psalm is an exclamation of faith (v. 25):

Whom have I in heaven but thee?
And there is nothing upon earth that I desire besides thee.

Psalm 74: God's House in Ruins

Here we have a congregation's lament at the destruction of the Temple. The historical reference is most likely Nebuchadnezzar's conquest of Jerusalem in 586 BC (2 Kings 25). However, some apply the psalm to Antiochus Epiphanes' desecration of the Temple in 167 BC.

The People's Lament (74:1-3)

The people feel rejected and punished due to God's anger (v. 1). Pathetically, they ask God to remember them and Mount Zion, where once he dwelled on earth (v. 2). His sanctuary has been completely destroyed by the enemy (v. 3).

Destruction (74:4-8)

God's enemies (and Israel's) shouted (roared) with delight at their destructive power, putting up their own banners in his holy place (v. 4). Enemies' shouts replaced Israel's praise in the Temple. Then they hacked the Temple to pieces and set it afire (vv. 5-7). They burned every worship assembly place in Israel (v. 8).

No Prophet in the Land (74:9-11)

Even worse than the destruction of their capital and Temple was the silence of God. The voice of the prophets was no longer heard. There was no "word from the Lord." How long would such unbearable conditions continue (v. 10)?

God Is Still King (74:12-17)

God alone can save his people (v. 12). The poet then cited the mighty acts of God in the past. He brought order out of chaos at creation (vv.

13-14). God provided water in the wilderness and dried up the Jordan for Israel to enter Canaan (v. 15).

The Egyptians worshiped the sun, but the God of Israel made it (v. 16). He is the Lord of all creation (v. 17).

A Prayer for Remembrance and Redemption (74:18-23)

The poet prayed that God's people, helpless as doves, would not be given to the wild beasts (v. 19). He asked God to "have regard for thy covenant" (v. 20) and to "arise" and remember his people (vv. 22-23). Hosea compared God's people to doves (Hos. 7:11; 11:11).

God is the Lord of creation and of his people.

Psalm 75: God, the Divine Judge

This psalm is a liturgy used in worship at the Temple in Jerusalem. The people chanted verse 1. Its theme is the judgment of God. People who are successful consider themselves "self-made." We are also quick to judge others. This psalm should correct both of these wrong attitudes.

God's Acts (75:1)

The congregation will recount the "wondrous deeds" of the Almighty on their behalf. His intervention calls forth their thanksgiving.

God's Message (75:2-5)

A prophet probably recited these verses. God alone can judge fairly, for he knows fully the circumstances and what is in the heart of mankind (v. 2). He keeps the earth secure (v. 3).

God warns against human pride and boasting (v. 4). The "horn" was a symbol of animal strength. The wicked were proud of their power and were arrogant people (v. 5).

God's Judgment (75:6-8)

Divine judgment is depicted here as a bitter cup of wine (v. 8). It must be drained "down to the dregs" as punishment for evildoing. All people's lives are in the hand of Providence (v. 7).

In Praise of God (75:9-10)

A soloist or chanter here praised God for humiliating the wicked and exalting the righteous. God alone can judge, and his judgment is often surprising!

Psalm 76: When Wrath Turns to Praise

Like Psalms 46 and 48, this psalm celebrates God's presence on Mount Zion. It is also a celebration of divine deliverance and victory over Israel's enemies. The historical reference may be to King Hezekiah's victory over Sennacherib in 701 BC (2 Kings 18—19). However, it applies to God-given victory at any time.

God in Salem (76:1-6)

God has established his residence in Jerusalem. ("Salem" is another name for the city of peace. *Shalom* means peace in Hebrew.) There God destroyed the enemies' weapons of war. Both soldiers and war-horses were rendered helpless by the Lord.

Note the poetic verse of praise set in this context of conflict: "Glorious art thou, more majestic than the everlasting mountains" (v. 4).

God in Judgment (76:7-12)

God is terrible in his wrath (v. 7). Nothing and no one can withstand his anger. He comes from heaven in judgment, and the earth is gripped by fear (v. 8). But note that it is on behalf of the poor and the oppressed that divine judgment is exercised (v. 9).

"The wrath of men shall praise thee" (v. 10). Human wrath only adds to God's glory, for he overrules our schemes (Rom. 9:17). God is not frustrated by evil but defeats it.

The people are told to pay their vows and bring their gifts in gratitude and praise of God (v. 11).

Psalm 77: The Long View of Faith

In the hard times which followed Israel's return from Exile the psalmist called for historical perspective. They should recall God's past favors, such as the miracles of the Exodus. These gave the psalmist ground for hope as he anticipated God's future intervention on behalf of his people.

Present Trouble (77:1-10)

Here we have a heartrending lament, vividly presented. The poet cried aloud to God in prayer but felt that he was not heard. Day and night he sought relief (v. 2). He thought and meditated. He spent sleepless nights searching his spirit (v. 6).

God had been gracious to Israel in the past (v. 5). Would he now spurn her forever (v. 7)? Note the pathos in verses 8-10. Has God changed? Has he forgotten how to be gracious or forgotten his covenant promises? Has his anger frozen his compassion?

Future Hope Is Based on God's Previous Grace (77:11-20)

God is unique, the only true God. "What god is great like our God?" (v. 13*b*). In this passage the poet blended three mighty acts of God: creation, thunderstorms, and the Exodus from Egypt.

God exercised his creative power over chaos (v. 16). He led his people through the Red Sea (v. 19). His might is demonstrated in the fearsome thunderstorm with its cloudburst, thunder, lightning, and whirlwind. "The earth trembled and shook" (v. 18*b*).

God had been with their fathers in days past (Jacob and Joseph and their sons; Moses and Aaron). This gave the psalmist and his contemporaries comfort and hope. They, too, could trust God for the present and future. We need a similar perspective and faith. (See Jesus' counsel in Matt. 6:25-33 and John 14:18-27.)

Psalm 78: Lessons from History

The theme of this psalm is the repeated disobedience of God's people in spite of all his mighty acts on their behalf. It is presented as the riddle of rebellion. The psalmist took on the role of teacher. He drew his lessons from three great events in Israel's history: the Exodus from Egypt, the wilderness wanderings, and the conquest of Canaan. His purpose was that his readers might learn from the past mistakes of their ancestors. The psalm may well have been read at observances of Passover.

"Lest We Forget" (78:1-8)

The teacher asks for a hearing. He is about to recite "the glorious deeds of the Lord" (v. 4). God had commanded that each succeeding generation be taught (v. 5) lest they "forget the works of God" (v. 7). They must not be like "their fathers, a stubborn and rebellious generation." Instead of viewing the good old days through rose-colored glasses, the poet recited both God's grace and their ancestors' unfaithfulness (v. 8).

The Fathers' Rebellion (78:9-31)

This is a study in human ingratitude and abounding grace. Despite divine deliverance, the Israelites did not keep their covenant with God (v. 10). They soon forgot his miracles: the plagues on the Egyptians, safely crossing the Red Sea, guidance by day and night, and the provision of water in the desert (vv. 12-16). "They sinned still more against him" (v. 17). Incredible!

The Israelites "tested God" in the desert. In mockery they asked, "Can God spread a table in the wilderness? . . . Can he also give bread?" (vv. 19-20). They had a "what have you done for me lately?" attitude. God knew the insolence which was in their hearts and on their tongues. Still, he provided manna and quail. Note the poetic description of manna as "the grain of heaven" and "the bread of angels" (vv. 24-25).

God gave the people what they needed and wanted. But "while the food was still in their mouths" (v. 30) they were rebellious and complaining. God's anger was kindled, and he destroyed some of their choice young men. (See Num. 11:33-34.)

Sin Despite Grace (78:32-39)

As incredible as it sounds, "in spite of all this they still sinned" (v. 32). When punishment came they pretended to repent, but they were lying (v. 36).

God was still compassionate (v. 38). He remembered that "they were but flesh" (v. 39). He was aware of their humanity. They grieved God, tested him, provoked him, and rebelled against him (vv. 40-41)—all this in light of his gracious deliverance! In Egypt he had turned the Nile to blood, sent plagues of flies, frogs, locusts, and hail as with "a company of destroying angels" (v. 49). Finally, he had smote all the firstborn of Egypt (v. 54), and defeated the people who had previously occupied it (v. 55). This mighty backdrop of grace makes their ingratitude all the darker.

Their Response: Idolatry (78:56-66)

Did they keep the covenant cut at Mount Sinai once they were settled in the Promised Land? No. Their response was to adopt the idolatry of the Canaanites (v. 58)!

God's response was to forsake his dwelling place at Shiloh (v. 60). He allowed the ark of the covenant to fall into the hands of the foe (v. 61). Refer to 1 Samuel 4:1-22 for this account. But God finally defeated the Philistines (v. 66) under the leadership of Saul and David.

God's Choice (78:67-72)

In his grace God chose the tribe of Judah for his people (v. 68). He chose Mount Zion as the site of his presence, in the Temple (v. 69). He chose the shepherd boy, David, to become the shepherd of his people (v. 70). O the wonder of God's gracious choosing!

Man's rebellion and selfishness is as much a puzzle today as it was in antiquity. It seems that we cannot be content no matter how gracious God is toward us. We soon forget his benefits. How amazing is God! He knows us as we are and still loves us.

Psalm 79: National Calamity

The setting of this psalm appears almost certainly to be the Babylonian invasion of Judah in 587 BC. The Babylonians defiled the Temple and destroyed Jerusalem. (See Ps. 74, which is similar.) The destruction of their Holy City and the deportation of the Jews into Exile has been called "the Old Testament Passion Story." This psalm is a national lament. Jerusalem was considered to be impregnable.

Catastrophe (79:1-7)

The psalmist began by describing the basis of his lament. This work must have been composed very soon after the destruction of the city. The memory seems fresh in the mind of the poet. He simply cannot believe what has happened! Jerusalem was thought to enjoy divine protection.

The heathen who did not hold God in awe had ravaged the Temple and left Jerusalem in ruins (v. 1). The people of God were the victims of atrocities. The enemy did not even bury the dead (vv. 2-3). Those who did survive were mocked by their neighbors, who should have helped them. Their neighbors were the people of Edom, Ammon, and Moab (vv. 4,12).

"How long" will the Lord be angry (v. 5)? The poet prayed that God would turn his anger on the kingdoms who "devoured Jacob, and laid waste his habitation" (v. 7).

Fixing Blame (79:8-9)

Notice the shifts within the psalm. First, the psalmist lashed out against Judah's destructive enemies (vv. 1-7). Next he acknowledged that one reason for the calamity was "the iniquities of our forefathers" (v. 8). Finally, the poet came to acknowledge personal responsibility: "Deliver us, and forgive our sins, for thy name's sake!" (v. 9).

There is a healthy progression here. We tend to react much the same. First, we blame some abstract enemy: "the devil made me do it." Then we blame someone else: our parents or friends. Finally, we are honest enough to acknowledge our own responsibility for sin and judgment. Only then can we experience forgiveness.

"Help Us, O God" (79:10-13)

The poet cried for help for two reasons: the great need of God's people and the honor of God's name. The pagans were asking: "Where is their God?" (v. 10). Judah was wondering the same thing.

The prisoners and those "doomed to die" in verse 11 were probably the Judeans taken captive and carried away into Exile. They were literally called "the sons of death." He prayed that God would hear their "groans" and save them.

The psalmist asked sevenfold punishment for the nation's enemies (complete destruction, v. 12). Then the people of God would praise him forever.

Psalm 80: Shepherd of Israel

This is another psalm of lament. We cannot be sure of its historical setting. Perhaps it was written at the fall of the city of Samaria in 721 BC.

"O Shepherd of Israel" (80:1-3)

This title cuts two ways. It is a reminder of God's pastoral care of his people, but it also implies their dependence on him.

To say that God is enthroned above the cherubim means he invisibly inhabits the holy of holies. Cherubs were angelic figures atop the ark of the covenant (1 Kings 6:23-28). Between them was the mercy seat where God's presence was located on earth. The psalmist prayed that the Shepherd would stir up his strength and save his people.

"O Lord of Hosts" (80:4-7)

This term literally means Lord of armies—Israel's and the angelic warriors of heaven. God's wrath had given his people tears to drink (v. 5). They experienced the scorn of both their enemies and their neighbors (v. 6).

"A Vine Out of Egypt" (80:8-19)

The poet depicted Israel as a young vine God took from Egypt and transplanted in Canaan. The figure of God's people as a vine is also used in Isaiah 5, Ezekiel 15, John 15 (by Jesus).

Unless a vine fulfills its purpose of bearing grapes, it is worthless. Jesus taught that unless believers abide in him, they "can do nothing" (John 15:5).

The transplanted vine, Israel, was very prosperous. It took deep root and filled the land (v. 9). Its branches reached from the sea to the Euphrates River. That was the extent of David and Solomon's kingdom (vv. 10-11).

But something happened. Because of the people's unfaithfulness, God broke down the protective wall surrounding Israel. Thieves could pluck their fruit, and wild boars could get in and root up the vine (vv. 12-13). These verses constitute a vivid metaphor of what was happening. The vine was being destroyed (v. 16).

The psalmist prayed for God's favor and blessing on the king (v. 17) and the people. He asked the Lord to: "Give us life . . . restore us . . . let thy face shine" upon us (vv. 18-19). He promised that they would continue to worship and serve the Lord. The absence of God was temporary. "They knew that the only real cure for their ills lay in the gift of the Presence of God."[1]

Note

1. John Durham, *The Broadman Bible Commentary* (Nashville: Broadman Press, 1971), vol. 4, p. 338.

Psalm 81: A Thanksgiving Sermon

Here we have a call to praise, "sing aloud to God" (v. 1), and a prophetic warning (vv. 11-16). The occasion for the psalm's use in worship was the autumn Feast of Tabernacles. It was the harvest festival, somewhat comparable to our Thanksgiving Day observance.

The first part of the psalm is a celebrative thanksgiving hymn (vv. 1-5*b*). The second half is a prophetic message (vv. 5*c*-16).

The Thanksgiving Hymn (81:1-5*b*)

The psalm begins with a colorful call to praise. It includes singing, shouting, and instrumental music. The trumpet (v. 3) was the *shofar* or ram's horn. Their autumn celebration was at the ordinance or command of God (v. 4). It was a joyous occasion.

The Thanksgiving Sermon (81:5c-16)

The message was given by a prophet who spoke for God to Israel. He rehearsed the highlights of Hebrew history. God had delivered them from burdensome toil and bondage in Egypt (vv. 6-7). He had answered them in the thunder from Mount Sinai (v. 7; Ex. 19:19). God had tested them at the waters of Meribah in the wilderness (Ex. 17:1-7).

Next, the prophet reminded his listeners of the Law of God. They were not to serve any "strange god" (v. 9; Ex. 20:3). And they were always to remember: "I am the Lord your God" (v. 10; Ex. 20:1-2). The children of Israel owed God their full allegiance for delivering them from slavery in Egypt. Even so, Christians owe their first loyalty to God through Jesus Christ for their deliverance from bondage to sin.

The Israelites were disobedient, choosing to go their own headstrong way (vv. 11-12). Thus God gave them their way and left them to their own devices. (See Rom. 1:24-32 for a parallel passage.) Still, God pled for them to obey him and be blessed (vv. 13-16).

Even in the midst of their harvest celebration the people needed to hear this warning. Let us remember the source of our prosperity and blessings—and be truly grateful. Heaven help us when we get to the point where we have no desire for God (v. 11). That is indeed a dangerous spiritual state. May God teach us both trust and genuine gratitude.

Psalm 82: Judge of Heaven and Earth

Interpreters of this psalm debate the identity of the "gods" (v. 1). Are they human judges? Then how do they appear in heaven? Are they angels? Then do angels die like men (vv. 6-7)? The best explanation seems to be that this psalm is an illustration of the First Commandment: "You shall have no other gods before me" (Ex. 20:3). Israel's great spiritual problem was idolatry—worshiping the pagan gods of their neighbors.

The Heavenly Court (82:1-4)

In a flight of imagination the psalmist saw the heathen gods assembled before the throne of God (v. 1). He accused them of being unjust and of showing partiality to the wicked (v. 2). They did not deal fairly with the weak, the destitute, and those who were oppressed (vv. 3-4). Injustice on earth is a result of serving false gods who do not have the high ethical standards of the Lord God (the Ten Commandments).

The Judgment of the Loving God (82:5-8)

Pagan gods are not enlightened or intelligent (v. 5). Neither are they immortal; they die with the men and women who serve them (vv. 6-7). Who in the world today worships Zeus, Venus, or Thor? No nation ever rises above the ethical level of its gods, its highest loyalty. Pagans and false gods alike die.

In verse 8 the worshipers acknowledge God as the real Judge of the earth, to whom all nations belong. The point of the psalm is that all pagan gods are nothing but man-made deities. People may call them gods, but they die with the culture. There is but one living God. He alone can judge people correctly, and we must serve him.

Psalm 83: Enemies of God

Israel aways had an abundant supply of enemies, as the long list in this psalm indicates. Since the Hebrews were God's chosen people, their enemies were his. Thus the poet could pray vividly for God to shame and destroy those nations who opposed Israel.

It appears that we have an historical collection of Israel's enemies listed here. Not all of these foes existed at the same time. However, the reference to Assyria in verse 8 would date the psalm around the last half of the eighth century BC. The Assyrian Empire came to prominence under the leadership of King Tiglath-pileser III.

A National Crisis (83:1-8)

The psalmist pled for God's attention to Israel's plight (v. 1). Their enemies, and his, had formed a deadly conspiracy. They plotted to wipe out the nation (vv. 4-5).

An impressive "enemies list" follows in verses 6-8. Edom, Moab, and Ammon were nations across the Jordan River and Dead Sea, east of Israel. Philistia was to the southwest, along the Mediterranean coast, in the area of the present-day Gaza Strip. Tyre was a city-state on the seacoast to the north. Other groups included warlike bedouin tribes from the desert. Assyria was a mighty empire to the north, bent on conquest. Israel was in military danger, its very existence threatened.

A Curse on Their Enemies (83:9-18)

The poet asked the Lord to do to his enemies what had been done to past foes. Then he gave some concrete examples. God had destroyed the Canaanites by the leadership of Deborah and Barak (Judg. 4—5). He had crushed the Midianites with Gideon's band of 300 soldiers (Judg. 7—8). The Lord had dealt a humiliating defeat to King Jabin and his general Sisera (Judg. 4). Their bodies were left unburied (v. 10). Israel's enemies had tried to take "the pastures of God" for themselves (v. 12).

Next, the psalmist prayed a vivid curse of natural disasters on his enemies: a whirling dust storm in which they would be blown "like chaff before the wind" (v. 13), a lightning-started forest fire which would set the mountains ablaze (v. 14), and a terrifying storm and hurricane from which they could not escape.

He prayed that the nation's enemies would be put to shame (vv. 16-17) and that the name of the Most High God would be vindicated.

There is a danger in identifying our enemies as the enemies of God. More than once, Christian countries have gone to war claiming that God was clearly on their side. However, tiny Israel was an island of faith in a sea of pagan nations. The enemies who threatened the Chosen People were, indeed, God's enemies, too. The psalmist's prayer shows a vivid imagination.

Psalm 84: At Home with God

"How lovely is thy dwelling place." Thus begins this memorable hymn of the Lord's house. It has inspired poets and musicians across the years. The psalmist celebrated the joy of worship in the Lord's presence, not simply the beauty of Solomon's Temple.

The poet is a pilgrim en route to the autumn festival (at the time of the early rains in October, v. 6). He longs for the experience of celebrative worship. He envies those who serve in the Temple full-time —even the birds that nest there. The "highways to Zion" are happy ways.

The psalm contains three Beatitudes (vv. 4-5,12).

Happy Are Those Who Dwell in the House of God (84:1-4)

The poet loves and longs for "the courts of the Lord" with his whole being—his soul, heart, and flesh (v. 2). Even the sparrow and swallow are at home in the Lord's house. So is the poet! He declares his personal faith in "my King and my God" (v. 3).

Blessed are the priests and musicians who serve in the Temple (v. 4).

Happy Are the Pilgrims En Route to Zion (84:5-9)

Not only are those who serve at the Temple blessed; so are the worshipers who come as pilgrims to the festival (v. 5). The early autumn rains are refreshing the land, after months of drought (v. 6). God's people go "from strength to strength" (v. 7). His presence is the source of their renewal.

The poet recited his prayers for the king in verses 8-9.

Happy Are Those Who Trust in the Lord (84:10-12)

Note the poetic beauty of verse 10. Vice-President Alben Barkley (of Harry Truman's administration) was stricken and died while reciting this verse during a speech. The "doorkeeper" at the Temple was probably the janitor. One day spent in the most lowly service in this sacred place was better than a thousand days anyplace else!

God was the psalmist's "sun"—his light and warmth. The Lord was his "shield"—his protection and providence. God gives those who "walk uprightly" his favor, honor, and prosperity (v. 11).

Blessed, indeed, is the person who trusts in the Lord! (v. 12). Those who serve in the Temple and those who worship there are blessed. But so is everyone who loves and lives for God.

A Christian often loves the church's building, its worship, and fellowship, as the Hebrew poet loved the Temple. We, too, have our sacred spots. We tend to associate God with the places where he has been most real in our experience. We do not worship those places but God whom we encounter there. We, too, are at home with God.

Psalm 85: "Revive Us Again"

The setting of this psalm appears to be just after the return of the Jews from Exile in Babylon. That would have been in the time of Zechariah and Haggai. The Exile was considered a judgment of God on the Hebrews for their idolatry and iniquity. That was the theme of the eighth-century BC prophets.

God's Favor in Times Past (85:1-3)

God had restored the fortunes of his people. In 538 BC they returned to their homeland under the kindness of Cyrus, the Persian conqueror of Babylon. This was taken as a sign of God's forgiveness and grace. The Lord restored, forgave, and pardoned them, withdrawing his wrath. Recall God's past grace to you.

Lord, Do It Again in Present Times (85:4-7)

Their present status was not as bright as the expectations of the prophet of the Exile (Isa. 40—66). The long-neglected land was poor, and times were hard. They were rebuilding their capital and Temple, but it lacked the glory of Solomon's day.

The people prayed that God would revive them again and restore the nation to its former greatness. The psalmist must have had in mind their spiritual health, as well as their political security (v. 7).

What are our present spiritual needs?

Expectations for the Future (85:8-13)

This section of the psalm must have been recited by a worship leader, a priest or prophet. It gave assurance of God's future grace toward his people: "He will speak peace to his people" (v. 8).

Note the poetic beauty of verses 10 and 11:

> Steadfast love and faithfulness will meet;
>> righteousness and peace will kiss each other.
> Faithfulness will spring up from the ground,
>> and righteousness will look down from the sky.

There is perfect balance here. The thoughts are similar to Isaiah 40—66.

God will grant his peace (shalom) and his salvation to those who trust in him.

The Temple of Zerubbabel was completed in 516 BC and enhanced by King Herod in Jesus' generation. But the ultimate realization of God's glory in the midst of his people came with the incarnation of God in Christ (John 1:14).

What do you expect of God in the future?

Psalm 86: "Thou Art My God"

We have an unusual structure in this psalm. It begins with a lament or plea for help, proceeds to thanksgiving, and then returns to lament.

A Prayer for Deliverance (86:1-7)

The poet pleaded for God to hear him. He saw himself as being poor and in need of divine aid. He was "godly" in that he was a man of devout faith. This is not a claim to be morally perfect. He confessed his faith, saying: "Thou art my God" (v. 2).

The psalmist described God in the lament as being good, forgiving, and loving. He had a clear view of the character of God. He was confident that his needs could be met by the one to whom he prayed.

A Note of Praise (86:8-13)

The God of Israel is not to be compared with the pagan deities: "There is none like thee . . . O Lord" (v. 8). God is the father of all the nations who will one day acknowledge his lordship (v. 9; Isa. 66:23).

The poet sang his praise and thanksgiving to God for his instruction, might, and "steadfast love toward me" (v. 13). In the past the Lord had delivered him from death (Sheol).

A Cry for Help (86:14-17)

The plea for help was renewed. The psalmist was despised for his faith by "insolent . . . ruthless men." He asked for divine favor and vindication, an often-repeated theme in the Psalter.

Though the poet suffered due to his faithfulness, he found in God the resources to meet his needs. Today the believer may be misunderstood and ridiculed for his faith. But his consolation comes through fellowship with God in earnest prayer.

Psalm 87: "Glorious Things of Thee Are Spoken"

Mankind has always been fascinated with cities, from the oldest to the newest. Cities are both beautiful and horrible, loved and feared. The faithful of three world religions look to Jerusalem as one of the world's most fascinating cities.

This psalm is an ode to the City of Zion (Jerusalem). An ancient exile wrote: "If I forget you, O Jerusalem, let my right hand wither!" (Ps. 137:5). The author of the Apocalypse reported: "And I saw the holy city, new Jerusalem, coming down out of heaven from God" (Rev. 21:2).

Jerusalem is more than a city with a fascinating history. It is also a symbol of our hunger for God and home and immortality.

This psalm inspired John Newton's great hymn, "Glorious Things of Thee Are Spoken." It celebrates the joy of our spiritual citizenship. Jerusalem is the mother of believers everywhere.

The City of God, Zion (87:1-3)

The poem begins with a hymn of praise to Jerusalem. God established and loves it. He chose to dwell with people in this city of international reputation (v. 3). Think of the great men whose lives have had Jerusalem as a setting: King David and Solomon, Isaiah and Jesus. It is without doubt a glorious place. Jesus worshiped there, wept over it, died, and arose outside its city wall.

The Mother of All Believers, Zion (87:4-6)

People in all lands who know God look to Jerusalem as their spiritual mother. Pilgrims came there to worship from Egypt (Rahab), Babylon, Philistia, and Phoenicia (Tyre). Every believer is a citizen of two cities, his own and Jerusalem.

God is also the God of all the nations. He will bless people by their faith, which had its origin in Zion. God keeps a record of his own (v. 6). One day "every knee should bow, in heaven and on earth and under the earth, and every tongue confess that Jesus Christ is Lord, to the glory of God the Father" (Phil. 2:10-11).

The new birth marks us as spiritual natives of Zion.

The Source of All Spiritual Blessings, Zion (87:7)

The faith in God represented by Jerusalem is the "spring" from which all blessings flow. This final verse shows praise in the worship of singers and dancers in the Temple.

The new Jerusalem is the symbol of the ultimate triumph of the kingdom of God and the unity of people from all nations in the family of God. "One cannot deny his birthright any more than he can choose it. And this is a cause for praise."[1]

Note

1. John Durham, *The Broadman Bible Commentary* (Nashville: Broadman Press, 1971), vol. 4, p. 350.

Psalm 88: Cry from the Depths

This has been called "the saddest psalm." It is a cry of agony by one who felt cut off from God. He saw no hope in this world or the next—and still he prayed. Durham calls the psalm "one long desperate groan."[1]

Prayer in Suffering (88:1-12)

The poet had prayed continually, by day and night (v. 1). Yet he was on the brink of death. (Sheol in v. 3 and the Pit in v. 6 are the same, the abode of the dead. The shadowy spirits who dwell there are called "shades" in v. 10.)

In addition to his illness, he suffered the rejection of his friends (v. 8). But the greatest agony was that he felt cut off from God, forsaken by the Eternal (v. 5).

The psalmist put four rhetorical questions to the Almighty: Does God perform miracles among the dead? Do the spirits of the dead praise God? Is God's steadfast love proclaimed in the grave? Is God's salvation celebrated "in the land of forgetfulness"? (vv. 10-12). The answer to each question was no, as far as the psalmist knew.

"Lord, Why the Darkness?" (88:13-18)

Instead of turning to praise or expressing hope for the future, the poet continued his lamentation. He prayed early in the morning (v. 13). Still, he felt cut off and under the judgment of God (v. 14). His illness dated from his youth (v. 15). Perhaps he had never known what it was to be well.

The poem is a dirge of dark despair due to the poet's extended illness, social rejection, and feeling of spiritual judgment. It shows the true feelings of the psalmist. Faith can confront mysterious suffering; and though the individual may die, the believing community lives on in hope.

Note

1. John Durham, *The Broadman Bible Commentary* (Nashville: Broadman Press, 1971), vol. 4, p. 350.

Psalm 89: God's Covenant with David

The setting of this royal psalm is a time of national crisis. It was probably used in Hebrew worship in various times of trouble, to recall God's promises.

The Preface (89:1-4)

The poet sang of God's "steadfast love" and "faithfulness." These words appear throughout the psalm. He celebrated God's covenant promise to his servant David and to his successors (v. 4).

God's Power as Creator and Sustainer (89:5-18)

The Lord is incomparable. No one in the councils of heaven or on earth is like the "Lord God of hosts" (v. 8). He has great power and might, but he is also faithful and dependable.

God rules the raging sea and at creation overcame the sea dragon of chaos (Rahab in v. 10). He is the owner of heaven and earth because he made them. Tabor and Hermon are mountains created by God. The "festal shout" of verse 15 was the congregational response. "Horn" in verse 17 is a symbol of strength. The king was God's "shield" to protect his people (v. 18).

The Davidic Covenant (89:19-37)

God's agreement with his servant King David was referred to in verse 3. Now the covenant is elaborated. It was God who gave David the crown and anointed him king (vv. 19-20).

The "faithful one" to whom God spoke in a vision was the prophet Nathan (v. 19; 2 Sam. 7:4,17). God promised David victory over his foes (vv. 22-23). The theme of God's "faithfulness and steadfast love" is reintroduced (v. 24). God promised to exalt David's strength (horn, v. 24). His kingdom would extend from the Mediterranean Sea to the Euphrates River (v. 25). God would adopt David as his son and make him the mightiest king on earth (v. 27). His lineage would be established forever (v. 29).

The covenant was a two-way street. David's descendants must obey God's law. If they failed to do so, God would punish them—but he would not forget the covenant promise (vv. 32-33).

Has God Forsaken His Covenant? (89:38-51)

The Davidic king has been defeated in battle. His conquest was most humiliating. He lost his crown and throne. The city walls were breached. He was held up to scorn. His enemies triumphed. The king was prematurely old and filled with shame.

In a royal lament the king asked: "How long will thy wrath burn like fire?" (v. 46). The poet appealed again to the steadfast love and faithfulness of God (v. 49). These were the nation's hope. These terms occur five and seven times in the psalm.

Verse 52 is a doxology to Book III of the psalms, not part of Psalm 89.

Psalm 90: God Is Eternal—Mankind Is Mortal

The theme here is God's eternity and mankind's mortality. God is infinite, and humans are finite. God is mighty; humanity is frail. God is holy; people are sinners. This psalm inspired Isaac Watts's famous hymn "O God, Our Help in Ages Past." Here faith deals with the brevity of human life.

God's Eternity and Man's Transience (90:1-12)

The opening line sets the tone of faith. The poet celebrated God's eternity, which predated creation itself. The mountains were considered the oldest part of the earth. The psalmist compared creation to birth (v. 2). Some Bible versions translate the name of God as "the Eternal."

It is God who turns man back to dust (v. 3; Gen. 2:7; 3:19). We are always measuring time, but to God a thousand years is equal to only part of one night (v. 4). The brevity of human life is compared to a flood, a dream, and grass, which are short-lived (vv. 5-6).

Persons die due to sin (vv. 7-9; Rom. 6:23). They die with a sigh. If they are fortunate and strong, they may live to be seventy or eighty. Such must have been exceptional when the life expectancy was half that. But even eighty years is not long enough—and they are filled with "toil and trouble" (v. 10). The important thing is for people to live wisely and well, with a sense of purpose (v. 12).

A Prayer for God's Blessings (90:13-17)

The people asked divine favor that their short lives might have meaning. They pled for joy and for God to "establish . . . the work of [their] hands" (v. 17).

Ancient mankind was helpless in the face of death and the indelible nature of his sin. Only the redemption and hope Christ gives can make both life and death meaningful. God, who is eternal, has made us in his image. He has set eternity in the heart of people. That longing can never be satisfied in seventy or eighty years. Only faith can make life something more than "a tale told by an idiot, full of sound and fury, signifying nothing" (Shakespeare, *Macbeth*, V,v.).

Psalm 91: Promise of Protection

This eloquent poem is a dramatic conversation used in worship. The first two verses were given by the worship leader. They state the theme: those who trust in God enjoy his protection. Next, the chorus or congregation responded (vv. 3-13). Finally, we have an oracle, read by a prophet, which represents God's promise of his presence (vv. 14-16).

The Theme (91:1-2)

God protects the person who cleaves to him in love. This section contains four different Hebrew names for deity: the Most High, the Almighty, the Lord, and God. God's "shelter" and "shadow" are ways of describing his protection. The metaphor used here is the shadow of his wings (v. 4) like a mother bird guarding her young.

The Response (91:3-13)

Next, the choir listed the ways in which God protects those who depend on him. The "snare of the fowler" represents man-made trouble, while "pestilence" may stand for dangers from nature.

Note the timely balance in verses 5 and 6: "the terror of the night . . . the arrow . . . by day . . . the darkness . . . [and] noonday." These are vivid phrases. Protection is given God's own, even in battle (v. 7). In verses 11 and 12 we find guardian angels. This is a beautiful promise. Recall that Satan tried to misapply it when he tempted Jesus (Luke 4:10-11).

Danger is described in terms of snakes and lions in verse 13.

God Speaks (91:14-16)

The oracle confirms the promise of divine protection. It begins by saying: "Because he cleaves to me in love . . ." (v. 14). God promised deliverance, an answer to his prayers (v. 15), and his presence in times of trouble. He also held out the hope of honor and long life (v. 16).

This psalm is not an excuse for arrogance. That is the kind of idea which comes from the devil. It speaks of faith that makes us feel secure in the presence of the Father.

Psalm 92: "It Is Good to Give Thanks"

This is a psalm of joy by one who believes in God's providence and justice—and has experienced it. The righteous have been rewarded and the wicked punished. This constitutes a call to praise. The psalm begins and ends with God.

Introductory Hymn (92:1-4)

The psalmist's joy spilled forth in a hymn of praise and thanksgiving. He pointed up the Lord's steadfast love and faithfulness. Believers can count on the Lord to keep his promises and to bless them. The poet praised God with musical instruments: the lute, harp, and lyre. He also sang for joy. His praise was continual—morning and night.

Destruction of the Wicked (92:5-11)

God's purposes and works are so great that sinners cannot understand them (vv. 5-6). Though the wicked grow like weeds, they will be cut down. Their doom is sure (v. 7).

The psalmist had been given strength "like that of the wild ox," and his enemies had been defeated (vv. 9-10). He had been anointed with the perfumed oil used on festive occasions. That was still another expression of his joy and praise.

Blessing of the Righteous (92:12-15)

Those who trust in God prosper. Using the metaphor of trees, the psalmist declared that "the righteous flourish like the palm tree," which can be fruitful. And they are as stately as the cedars in Lebanon. Planted in the presence of the Lord, they flourish. Even in old age they are still vigorous and bear fruit.

The poet confessed his faith, saying: "The Lord . . . he is my rock" (v. 15). The psalm is one of joyous gratitude to God.

Psalm 93: The Lord Is King

There are six enthronement psalms (47,93, and 96—99). This shortest one celebrates the kingship of God: "The Lord reigns." He is sovereign over all creation, including nature and mankind. And he is king from all eternity.

The psalmist pictured the Almighty as "robed in majesty . . . [and] strength" (v. 1). He is king of the world which he established and controls. His is an everlasting kingdom (v. 2). The ultimate will of God shall be realized with certainty.

The floods and storm of verses 3-4 are a favorite Hebrew symbol of chaos and trouble. At creation the Lord showed himself to be "mightier" than chaos and the deep. He is the God of peace and not confusion. He stills the storm as Jesus did on the Sea of Galilee.

The psalmist confessed his faith in the sovereign might of God. The Lord is both powerful and dependable. We can trust his word and his character (v. 5). "Praise to the Lord, the Almighty, the King of creation!" Celebrate his sovereignty. God is in control. We need not fear him but may join in the poet's praise.

Psalm 94: God of Vengeance

This psalm constitutes a prayer for justice. The wicked appear to be getting away with a series of crimes. Even worse, the ungodly are convinced that "the Lord does not see" (v. 7) what they are doing. The poem is a petition for God to judge evil and punish evildoers.

The psalmist takes comfort in three facts: 1. God as creator of humanity and his teacher (v. 10) is aware of evil in the world and will assure that justice is done. 2. There are still those who are "upright in heart" (v. 15). The world has not been given over completely to evil. 3. God has upheld him in times of need in the past. This constitutes a consolation in the poet's present crisis (vv. 18-19).

"The Judge of the Earth" (94:1-15)

The psalmist appealed to God, the righteous judge, for justice. The wicked are indicted in these verses. They are proud and boastful. They crush and oppress others, especially the fatherless who have no one to defend them (v. 6). They are practical atheists, as well (v. 7).

How foolish! Would the Creator who made the ear and eye himself be unable to hear or see? (V. 9 is vivid poetry and a strong argument.) God knows the very thoughts of people—and their frailty (v. 11). Fortunate is the person whom God corrects, for he learns by being chastened (v. 12; see also Prov. 3:11-12; Job 5:17; Heb. 12:5-6).

The psalmist was convinced that God would not forsake his own. Justice would be done (vv. 14-15).

The Lord Stands Up for Us (94:16-23)

It is God who will judge the wicked; God will defend his own (vv. 16-17). God had kept the poet's foot from slipping in the past (v. 18). Thus he can be trusted for the future. This assurance is a source of comfort to us as well as to the ancient poet (v. 19).

Wicked officials were not acting on God's orders or with his blessing (vv. 20-21). The psalmist trusted the Lord as his defense and place of safety (v. 22). God would deal decisively with the wicked in due course (v. 23). They would not continue to get away with their mischief. No one is exempt from moral law or immune to judgment. Many have discovered this truth despite their assumptions to the contrary.

Psalm 95: Listen to His Voice

The three great teachings of Israel's faith are found in this psalm: 1. God is the Creator of the world and of mankind. 2. God redeemed his Chosen People by the Exodus from Egypt. 3. Therefore, they have a moral and ethical responsibility to live in obedience to his laws.

The psalm includes a call to worship and a hymn (vv. 1-7a) and a prophetic oracle or sermon (vv. 7b-11). The passages in Hebrews 3:7-11 and 4:3-11 are built on the warnings of this psalm.

A Hymn to God, the Great King (95:1-7b)

The hymn begins with a majestic call to worship (vv. 1-2). Note the importance of music and singing in Hebrew worship. Next, the poet celebrated the greatness of God as Creator. The Lord is "a great king above all gods" (v. 3). This does not mean that the psalmist believed in the existence of pagan deities. Rather, he was emphasizing the uniqueness of the one true God.

The deepest parts of the earth and the tallest peaks of the mountains belong to God. He made and owns both the sea and the dry land (vv. 4-5).

The worshipers in the Temple were told to kneel before the Lord. Normally, Jews stood to pray. Bowing was a sign of devotion—"he is our God, and we are . . . his . . . sheep" (v. 7).

"O That Today You Would Hearken to His Voice!" (95:7c-11)

This section constitutes a call to hear and give heed to God's word. At this point the psalm was probably recited by a cultic prophet as a word from the Lord. It is a warning: Do not repeat the hardhearted unbelief of your forefathers. They disgusted God and were doomed to wander in the wilderness for a generation (v. 10).

Those in the Temple when this hymn was sung were called to worship and warned about unbelief. If they disobeyed they would forfeit their "rest" in the favor of the Lord (v. 11). As noted, the author of the Epistle to the Hebrews sounded this warning for Christians, as well. Jesus requires obedience as well as the profession of our faith (see Luke 6:46-49).

Psalm 96: The Lord Is King and Judge

Psalms 47, 93, and 96-99 celebrate God as sovereign King over all

people. He judges the earth fairly. The style of Psalms 96—99 indicates
that they had the same author. They are similar in thought to Isaiah
40—66. They show the kingdom of God in its past, present, and future
tenses.

"Sing to the Lord a New Song" (96:1-6)

The people at worship were invited to sing a new song (this psalm).
"All the earth" was invited to join in (v. 1). Notice the verbs: *"sing . . .
bless* his name . . . *tell* of his salvation . . . *declare* his glory among the
nations" (vv. 2-3).

God is great and not to be compared to empty idols (vv. 4-5). He is the
living God, Creator of both heaven and earth. Therefore, he is worthy of
our worship and honor (v. 6). Pagan gods are impotent. The Lord is
powerful.

Worship the Lord, Both Men and Nature (96:7-13)

The psalmist's hearers were invited to ascribe the glory due God's
name (v. 7). They were encouraged to worship him with their offerings
(v. 8). This invitation was extended in a missionary fashion to "all the
earth!" (v. 9).

The reference to worship "in holy array" recalled to mind the robes
worn by the priests. They reflected the joy of worship on festive occasions.

"The Lord reigns!" As surely as he established the world, one day evil
will be banished and God will establish justice (v. 10). This reflects great
faith on the part of the poet. It is also what the Christian fully expects to
happen once the kingdom of God comes in its completeness. Jesus, who
reigned from the cross, has been highly exalted. He now reigns with the
Father and will one day return in glory.

In a burst of poetic enthusiasm the psalmist called on nature to join in
the praise of God and his universal reign: heavens and earth are to rejoice; the sea is to roar and the fields exult; even the trees are to "sing for
joy" before the Lord (vv. 11-12). Nature, as well as mankind, is fallen
due to sin. Both are in the process of redemption. (See Isa. 11:6-10;
55:12-13; Rom. 8:19-25.) God is both universal King and the righteous
Judge (v. 13). Note the broad scope of his power: "the world."

Psalm 97: Lord of Light

This enthronement psalm depicts the Lord in mystery and might. He brings shame to those who worship idols (v. 7) and joy to those who worship himself (v. 8). Our morality is to be based on the holy character of God—not some shallow humanitarianism.

"The Lord Reigns" (97:1-5)

This is the theme of the enthronement psalms. Since God is in charge, "let the earth rejoice" (v. 1). The "coastlands" may be translated islands.

Note the mystery of God. "Clouds and thick darkness" surround him. His presence is veiled and mysterious (v. 2). No one fully sees and knows God except the Son.

Fire is the symbol of both judgment and blessing in verses 3-4. Fire proceeds from God to punish and destroy evil. Yet the poet contended that "his lightnings lighten the world." The earth trembles before its Maker, and "the mountains melt like wax" (v. 5). This sounds like a volcanic eruption.

Living God Vs. Empty Idols (97:6-9)

God reveals himself in both creation and in redemptive history. Still, there were those who worshiped graven images and "worthless idols" (see Jer. 10:14). Despite divine revelation of the loving Father, people continue to give their highest loyalty to things less than God. In what shape is your idol?

The angels in heaven ("gods" in vv. 7b, 9b) know better. So do believers in Mount Zion and Judah. They rejoice in the Lord (v. 8). He is the exalted King over all the earth (v. 9).

The People of God (97:10-12)

The Lord loves, preserves, and delivers "his saints" (v. 10). The poet has moved from the universal praise of God to the worship of God's covenant people.

"Light" is a symbol of divine blessing in this psalm (v. 11). "Light dawns" in the Hebrew is literally "light is sown." God's influence is not static but growing and pervasive in the life of the believer. Note its great significance in the Gospel of John. The people are admonished to rejoice and give thanks to the Lord (v. 12).

Our morality finds its foundation in the character of God. Because he is holy, we are called to be holy. Our attempt at human righteousness based on any standard less than the Ten Commandments is not worthy.

The veiled mystery of God's person and purpose is revealed in the words and works of Jesus. We strive to do what is right out of gratitude for his salvation. We want to know the mind of Christ and do the Father's will. Our objective is to please God.

Psalm 98: God as Victor

This is the only enthronement psalm which does not include the phrase "The Lord reigns." However, God is called "the King" in verse 6. It is divided into three sections of three verses each, as indicated by the paragraphs in the Revised Standard Version.

God's Victory in the Past (98:1-3)

God's mighty acts on behalf of his people caused them to sing a new song (v. 1). God had granted victory and salvation, vindicating Israel in the eyes of their enemies and "all the ends of the earth" (v. 3). God kept his covenant promises to the nation. This called forth their praise. Paul also promised that God will complete what he has begun in us (Phil. 1:6). This psalm is a song of victory which recalls the triumph of Easter for Christians.

God Is King in the Present (98:4-6)

. The people, led by their musicians, were called on to join in the praise of God. Indeed, "all the earth" was urged to "break forth into joyous song" (v. 4). Instrumental music accompanied their singing in praise of the Lord, the King (vv. 5-6).

God Will Judge with Equity in the Future (98:7-9)

The world of nature, as well as of humanity, was invited to praise (v. 7b). The sea will roar, the rivers (floods) will clap their hands, and the hills will "sing for joy" at God's righteous judgment. (See Ps. 96:11-13.) When the kingdom comes completely, righteousness will prevail. This truth constitutes a call to joy and praise.

Psalm 99: "God Is Holy!"

The enthronement motif occurs again: "The Lord reigns!" (v. 1). This psalm focuses on the holiness of God, which involves both his *pardon* of the sinner and his *punishment* of sin. The chorus of the psalm is repeated in verses 5 and 9: "Extol the Lord our God, and worship at his holy mountain (his footstool); for the Lord our God is holy!"

The Mighty King (99:1-5)

Both people and nature are called to tremble and quake before the Lord (v. 1). This means reverence for the Creator, not cringing fear before a cruel deity. God's name is not to be taken lightly, but seriously (v. 3). His perfection inspires reverence on the part of his imperfect creation.

God loves justice, and so should we (v. 4). The Temple in Jerusalem is called God's "footstool." Isaiah called the earth the Almighty's footstool (66:1).

Pardon and Punishment (99:6-9)

Although the Puritans made too much of God's punishment of evil, modern interpreters have come down on the side of divine love almost to the neglect of judgment. The psalmist struck a wise balance between these two activities of the Lord.

God strikes fear in those who do not believe but calls forth joy in those who place their trust in him. Evildoers fear the law with cause, but those who obey the law have nothing to fear from it.

Moses, Aaron, and Samuel were called "priests" by the psalmist (v. 6). They represented the people before the Lord. They prayed to him and he answered, revealing his will for the nation by giving his law ("statutes," v. 7).

The psalm was concluded with the chorus (v. 9), which may have been sung by the choir.

Psalm 100: Invitation to Praise

Mankind is called to thanksgiving, to celebrate God as Creator and King. Imagine a procession of worshipers approaching Jerusalem with its Temple gleaming in the sun. They sang the first three verses of Psalm 100 at the city gates. From within the Temple courtyard the choir answered antiphonally with verses 4-5.

This call to praise is based on the fact that the Lord alone is God (v. 3). He is our Creator, and we are his people. One of the most famous hymns in English, "All People That on Earth Do Dwell," is based on this psalm. The psalm's popularity is second only to that of Psalm 23.

Joy in God—Why We Worship

The Lord alone is God. He is One (Deut. 6:4). God is the Creator who made us. There are no self-made persons. God is our Shepherd or pastor.

He knows us and gives himself for us. God is good and completely dependable. "His steadfast love endures for ever" (v. 5).

Imperatives of Praise—How We Worship

The psalmist called on the worshipers to:
Shout—"Make a joyful noise to the Lord, all the lands!"
Worship—"Serve the Lord with gladness!"
Sing—"Come into his presence with singing!"
Know by experience that the Lord is our Creator.
"*Enter* his gates with thanksgiving and his courts with praise!"
"*Give thanks* to him and bless his name!"

The reason for our worship is beautifully stated in verse 5. For more than twenty centuries both Jews and Christians have used this simple psalm in joyous worship of God. It is a universal invitation to all the earth to praise him. He is God of both the universe and his people.

May God who has given us so much give us one thing more—a grateful heart.

Psalm 101: "With Integrity of Heart"

This psalm is the Davidic king's prayer and pledge. It holds up an ideal for all who serve in positions of authority in any age. Its focus is political ethics, an important commodity.

The Ruler's Integrity (101:1-4)

The king promised to value loyalty and justice (v. 1). He determined to walk with "integrity of heart," not giving place to anything base in his personal life (vv. 2-3). He would keep himself from evil, reward the righteous, and root out evil and corruption in public life (vv. 4-5). The king dedicated himself to goodness and personal integrity. Worship and ethics should be inseparable.

Ethics in Public Life (101:5-8)

The king did not try to separate personal ethics from public life. He vowed that he would not tolerate those who were slanderers, arrogant, deceitful, or liars. Such a promise could call for cleaning house in much of modern public service. A leader who has integrity will seek dependable persons to work with him. This psalm depicts a righteous person serving in public office. "Integrity" (v. 2) is the key word. ("Purity of heart" is *The New English Bible*'s translation.)

Psalm 102: In Times of Trouble

This is one of the individual laments called the "penitential" psalms. (See Pss. 6; 32; 38; 51; 130; 143.) It deals with the plight of the poet and the nation (illness and exile) in the light of God's eternal nature.

The Psalmist's Illness and Isolation (102:1-11)

The psalmist pleaded with God to hear and answer his prayer for deliverance (vv. 1-2). His days vanished like smoke. They were insubstantial. His body burned with fever (v. 3). His vigor wilted like grass, and he lost all appetite for food (v. 4).

The poet described his loneliness with the metaphor of lonely birds who inhabit wastelands: the vulture and owl (vv. 6-7). Added to his illness and isolation was the ridicule of his enemies (v. 8). Poetically, he said he had eaten ashes for bread and tears mixed with his drink (v. 9). He considered his suffering to be a punishment from God (vv. 10-11).

God Will Deliver and Restore (102:12-22)

This psalm appears to have been written during the Jewish Exile in Babylon. The poet appealed to the Lord to "have pity on Zion" (v. 13) and restore her. As a result, he wrote, "people yet unborn may praise the Lord" (v. 18). That promise was fulfilled. Generations of Jews have blessed the Lord for answering this prayer. God hears and delivers the oppressed (v. 20). People of all nations worship the Lord in gratitude (v. 22).

Eternal God (102:23-28)

The poet returned to writing of his distress but saw it in the light of God's eternity. God outlives all generations (v. 24). He laid the foundation of the earth long ago. Heaven and earth will one day wear out like old clothes and be cast aside—but God goes on forever: "thou art the same" (v. 27). God has always existed and always shall. In contrast, the world and mankind are transient. (Compare Heb. 1:10-12 in which Ps. 102:25-27 is quoted from the Greek translation of the Old Testament, the Septuagint.) It has been suggested that Psalm 103 is a companion poem which answers the thought in Psalm 102.

Psalm 103: "Bless the Lord"

The artful simplicity of this great psalm teaches that God knows mankind in his frailty and loves him still. It focuses on the brevity of human life and the eternal kingship of God.

This hymn of praise has inspired many Christian hymns, including "Praise, My Soul, the King of Heaven." It is a psalm of personal praise based on the experience of the poet. In all probability it was used as a solo in Hebrew worship.

Personal Praise (103:1-5)

The psalmist called on his soul to bless the Lord. By "soul" he meant his whole being—intellect, emotions, and spirit—not just some part of his person. God's holy name means his revealed character (v. 1).

Note God's benefits, his actions on our behalf: He forgives all our sins, heals our diseases, and redeems us from death. (The "Pit" is a synonym for Sheol, the abode of the dead.) More than that, we are the recipients of his steadfast love. He gives us long life and renews our youth like the eagle's (v. 5). Because the eagle moults each year, the ancients thought it took on new life—thus the poetic reference to youthful strength and renewal.

National Praise (103:6-18)

The psalm now celebrates divine blessings on the nation. God provides justice for the oppressed (v. 6). He is compassionate and merciful (vv. 7-8). His anger is not without limits, and he does not hold a grudge (v. 9).

God punishes his people when they sin, but not as much as their iniquity deserves. His punishment is tempered (v. 10). His steadfast love is limitless (v. 11), and he forgives our sins decisively (v. 12). God is a Father to his children, tender and understanding (vv. 13-14; see Gen. 2:7). He knows our frailty, vividly described in verses 15-16. Our weakness is contrasted with his everlasting love (v. 17). He wants us to "keep his covenant" (v. 18).

Praise from All Creation (103:19-22)

While God may dwell in the midst of his people, in the Temple, his throne is in the heavens (v. 19). He is king of heaven and earth. His kingdom is universal.

The poet calls on the angels as well as on mankind to "Bless the

Lord." Note that this phrase is repeated four times in poetic fashion in verses 20-22. The pattern of praise progresses from an individual to the congregation and the angels to the entire created order. Then the psalmist came back to his point of beginning. He concluded with the words "Bless the Lord, O my soul!"

This psalm constitutes a beautiful poetic call to praise for all people. We all benefit from the Father's undeserved grace (v. 10). Grace is God's extra in our life. God loves us as we are, even when we do not love ourselves. That is the most amazing miracle. Yet the truth is that our praise and gratitude are not automatic. They must be called forth. Never take for granted God's kindness, forgiveness, and mercy. They are his gracious extras!

Psalm 104: God's Mighty Work in Creation

This is a poem of sheer grandeur. It was the inspiration for the hymn "O Worship the King." It is a colorful paraphrase of the creation story (Gen. 1) and is similar to Job 38—41. Its theme is the greatness of God. The psalm is similar to a hymn to the sun written by Egyptian Pharaoh Amenhotep IV (also called Akhenaton) around 1350 BC. However, the theology is strikingly different. Pharaoh thought the sun was the creator, but the psalmist said that the sun is a part of the Lord's creation.

Beginning with the Heavens (104:1-4)

Both Psalms 103 and 104 begin and end with praise: "Bless the Lord, O my Soul." This section depicts God in his majesty and glory. He wears light as his mantle. The first thing created was light. Without it there would be no life. Light is also a symbol of the divine presence (Ex. 3:2; John 1:4-5; Rev. 21:23).

God's chariot is the clouds. He rides on the wings of the wind. The winds are his messengers; and the lightning bolts are his servants (v. 4). This verse is quoted in Hebrews 1:7. What vivid poetry! The same Hebrew word used here may be translated wind, breath, or spirit.

Moving to the Earth (104:5-30)

The earth was created at God's word and is subject to his control. When God spoke, the chaotic waters of the deep fled to their proper place (vv. 7-9). The winds and waves obey him (and his Son).

Streams and rain provide essential water for vegetation and animal life (vv. 10-13). Grass and crops provide food for people and animals. Wine makes people glad; olive oil is their cosmetic; and bread makes them strong (v. 15). These were the principal crops in Palestine.

God provides trees for the birds (v. 17) and mountains for the wild goats and burrowing badgers (v. 18). The moon marks the seasons (v. 19). Nighttime is for animals of prey (vv. 20-21) and daylight is for mankind's work (vv. 22-23).

"How manifold are thy works!" the psalmist exclaimed (v. 24). The sea is "great and wide," teeming with life, sailed by great ships, and the home of Leviathan, probably the whale (vv. 25-26).

God provides for his creatures (vv. 27-28). When he withholds his breath they return to dust (v. 29). Yet his Spirit can create new life. (On the new creation see Isa. 65:17; 66:22; 2 Pet. 3:13; Rev. 21:1.) Every living thing and person is dependent on God. He is the Author of life. It is his good gift to be received with gratitude.

A Doxology (104:31-35)

This is a lyrical prayer that God's glory will last forever. He takes great delight in creation. If a gardener finds his work rewarding, how much more must the Creator enjoy his handiwork?

The poet promised to sing God's praise as long as he lived (v. 33). He concluded the psalm with the self-admonition: "Bless the Lord, O my soul! Praise the Lord!" (v. 35). This psalm is an exciting personal testimony.

Psalm 105: Lord of History

The theme of this psalm is the history of salvation. It gives an account of God's mighty acts in the history of the Israelites from the time of Abraham to their settling in the Promised Land. The poet's purpose was to show how God had fulfilled his promise to Abraham and to his descendants. Those who read and hear the psalm are invited to "tell of all his wondrous works" (v. 2) and to "keep his statutes" (v. 45).

The first fifteen verses of Psalm 105 are quoted in the account of King David's bringing the ark of the covenant to Jerusalem (1 Chron. 16).

Remember God's Works and Sing Praise (105:1-6)

God's mighty acts and miracles on behalf of his Chosen People call forth their gratitude and praise. They are "his chosen ones!" (v. 6). This means they are God's elect. The divine choice requires their obedience (v. 45) as well as their praise.

The Patriarchs, God's Anointed Leaders (105:7-25)

The psalmist recounted God's deeds in the earliest times of Israel's history. He made an everlasting covenant with Abraham, Isaac, and Jacob (vv. 8-11). He promised them the land of Canaan for an inheritance (v. 11). This promise was given while they were still landless nomads (vv. 12-13). God protected them and made them the channels of his redemptive message and purpose ("prophets," v. 15).

God sent Joseph into Egypt ahead of his family and prior to the great famine. This proved providential. Joseph was tested and later exalted by Pharaoh. Still later, Israel came into Egypt (also called Ham in vv. 23,27). God was preparing his people for the Exodus.

Moses and Aaron, Leaders in Crisis (105:26-42)

These God-chosen leaders were used mightily to deliver the Hebrews from bondage. The psalmist cited eight of the plagues on Egypt, including the death of the firstborn (v. 36). The Hebrews brought booty out of Egypt in compensation for their enslavement (v. 37). After all that happened, the Egyptians were glad to see them go (v. 38).

God provided for his people in the desert: the pillars of cloud and fire, quail and "bread from heaven" (manna), as well as water from the rock (vv. 39-41). He kept his promise to his servant Abraham (v. 42).

The Reason for God's Deliverance (105:43-45)

God chose Israel to be his own people. He led them out of bondage with joy and singing. His providence brought them to the land of promise.

Note that God's grace called for the people's responsibility as well as their praise. He did all this so that they would "keep his statutes, and obey his laws" (v. 45). Divine election is double-edged. It involves both privilege and responsibility. (See Amos 3:2 and Luke 12:48.) God's call requires our response and faithfulness as well as our gratitude. Israel failed to be obedient, as we shall see in Psalm 106.

Psalm 106: A History of Sinfulness

Psalm 105 emphasizes God's faithfulness on behalf of his Chosen People. Psalm 106 recounts his people's unfaithfulness to God.

"Praise the Lord" (106:1-5)

The introduction to the psalm is a call to praise prompted by God's faithfulness and mighty acts on behalf of his people. The poet pronounced a blessing on those who act justly and obey the divine will (v. 3). In verses 4-5 the poet prayed that God might remember him and deliver him when the nation is delivered.

The Sins of Israel (106:6-46)

Israel's sins are related by the psalmist for forty verses: "Both we and our fathers have sinned" (v. 6). That is as true today as when the poet wrote it. He acknowledged both his forebears' failures and his own generation's responsibility. That is a mature understanding. Note the catalog of sins:

• They rebelled at the Red Sea (vv. 6-12). Still, God spared them and brought them safely across. Then they sang his praise.

• They murmured in the wilderness (vv. 13-15). They soon forgot the divine deliverance. Memory can be amazingly short.

• They were jealous of Moses and Aaron, their leaders (vv. 16-18). See Numbers 16.

• The Israelites worshiped the golden calf at Mount Sinai (Horeb, vv. 19-23). They exchanged the glory of the presence of God for a man-made idol—and the image of a beast at that. God would have destroyed them had it not been for Moses' intercession.

• Their disbelief when the spies returned from the Promised Land was a gross failure of faith (vv. 24-27).

• They took part in Moabite worship of Baal (vv. 28-31). It appears that this included a kind of ancestor worship (v. 28).

• At Meribah, Moses was rash and sinned (vv. 32-33). The result was that he was not permitted to enter the Land of Promise—a high penalty for his irreverence (Deut. 32:51-52).

• After the conquest of Canaan, the Hebrews joined in the worship of their neighbors' idols, polluting themselves (vv. 34-39). This even included human sacrifice (v. 37)!

• The period of the Judges was one of disobedience, punishment, and cries for relief, pardon, and deliverance (vv. 40-46). They repeatedly forgot the covenant, but God remembered it (v. 45).

A Concluding Prayer (106:47-48)

Verse 47 is a sentence prayer for salvation with the promise of praise.

Verse 48 is a doxology for Book IV of the Psalter. It blesses the Lord and calls for the people's response of praise and "Amen."

Psalm 107: Man's Name Is Trouble

Wisdom is born of trust in God's steadfast love. In Israel this trust was based on what God had done for his people in days past. His gracious acts of the past became bright promises of his future grace. God is worthy of our trust.

Psalm 8 teaches that man has worth; Psalm 107 shows that man is frail and subject to trouble.

A Call to Thanksgiving (107:1-3)

Let those who have experienced God's deliverance speak up. He formed the nation, bringing them to worship in the Temple.

Note how the refrain is repeated: "Let them thank the Lord for his steadfast love, for his wonderful works to the sons of men!" (vv. 8,15,21,31). It was sung antiphonally. The poet cited four troubles from which God delivered his people.

Man, the Pilgrim—God, Our Guide (107:4-9)

Men were rootless nomads, aimless wanderers, with no city to call home. They were suffering refugees who "cried to the Lord in their trouble" (v. 6). He led them to a city. Refrain (v. 8).

Man, the Prisoner—God, Our Deliverer (107:10-16)

The prison (v. 10) may be literal, or it may be "the prison house of sin." In both cases man is enslaved (v. 12). Mankind "cried to the Lord," (v. 13) and he brought them out, freed them, and pardoned them. Refrain (v. 15).

Man, the Sufferer—God, Our Physician (107:17-22)

Some were sin-sick and almost at "the gates of death" (vv. 17-18). They cried to the Lord, and he healed them (vv. 19-20). Refrain (v. 21).

Man, the Sailor—God, Our Pilot (107:23-32)

Reading verses 23-27 will almost make one seasick because they are so vivid. Sailors in distress found that their "courage melted," and they were "at wits' end."

They cried to the Lord, and he stilled the storm (as Jesus did on Galilee). The refrain occurs a final time (v. 31).

Epilogue (107:33-43)

God is Lord of both nature and the nations. He provides for the needy and punishes their oppressors (vv. 39-43).

The psalm's theme is God's dependable love. It is unchanging, unlimited, undeserved, and always available.

Psalm 108: A Composite

This psalm is a combination of materials from Psalms 57 and 60. The first five verses are quoted from Psalm 57:7-11 and verses 6-13 from Psalm 60:5-12. You may want to see the commentary on these earlier psalms from which this one was compiled.

Psalm 109: An Angry Prayer

Many commentators consider this the most severe of the "cursing psalms." The psalmist's theology obviously predates Jesus' teaching to "love your enemies" (Matt. 5:44). The poet was fully human, and we can identify with him, perhaps a bit too readily.

The Psalmist's Enemies (109:1-5)

The enemies had proved to be "wicked and deceitful" (v. 2). They attacked the psalmist "without cause" and returned for his love false accusations (vv. 3-4). They rewarded him with "evil for good" and "hatred for . . . love" (v. 5).

A Curse on His Enemies (109:6-19)

Some commentaries see this section as a curse upon the psalmist by his enemies, since the psalm changes from plural "them" to singular "him." Others consider this an unlikely interpretation.

The curses are bitter: may he be brought to trial and found guilty (vv. 6-7); may his life be short and his possessions be seized (see Acts 1:20, where verse 8b was applied to Judas); may his children be orphans and his wife a widow (v. 9); may his family be left destitute (vv. 10-12); may his children not survive and his name be forgotten (v. 13); may he be punished for the sins of his ancestors (v. 14).

The poet prayed that his enemy might be clothed in curses and soaked to the bone by them (vv. 18-19). This is a harsh prayer.

An Appeal for Help (109:20-31)

The poet turned from cursing his enemy to asking God's help for himself. His own plight was pitiful: he was poor and needy (v. 22). Poverty is dehumanizing. Poverty does not equal piousness. The psalmist's life was almost gone "like a shadow at evening" (v. 23). His body was weak and gaunt, and he was the object of scorn (vv. 24-25). Therefore, he cried out for help (v. 26).

Verses 29 and 19 express a similar thought. He asked that his enemy be brought to shame and dishonor.

In conclusion the poet promised to praise God among the worshipers in the Temple (v. 30). God is a present help to those who are in need (v. 31).

What are we to make of this cursing psalm? Note the poet's honesty. There are times when we, too, feel like lashing out at our enemies. John Durham wrote: "We may never be able to love our enemies until we admit . . . how easy it is to curse them."[1]

Note

1. John Durham, *The Broadman Bible Commentary* (Nashville: Broadman Press, 1971), vol. 4, pp. 395-396.

Psalm 110: King and Priest

This is an early royal psalm used in worship at the coronation of Davidic kings. Oracles from the Lord were addressed to the king by a priest or prophet. Compare this psalm with Psalm 2.

What the Psalm Meant Originally

The psalmist pointed out that:

• The source of the king's authority was God (vv. 1-2a; Rom. 13:1). This was not a doctrine of the divine right of kings.

• The king stands in a special relationship to the Lord (v. 3). The people, therefore, would offer themselves freely in the king's service.

Poetically, the morning is said to be mother of the life-giving dew.

• The king also had a priestly function. He was God's representative to the people (v. 4).

• The king's enemies would be overcome, with God's help (vv. 1c,2b,5-7).

To be at God's right hand is to be in a place of honor and authority. Note that the two oracles from the Lord are in quotation marks in the Revised Standard Version (vv. 1,4b). The king was God's son by adoption. Jesus was fully the Son of God.

Melchizedek was the priest and king of Salem (Jerusalem) in Abraham's day (see Gen. 14:18-20). The Davidic kings and the Messiah were in that long line of priest-kings. They represented God to his people. God will judge the nations "on the day of his wrath" (v. 5).

What the Psalm Meant to Early Christians

The early church saw the references in this psalm as being clearly messianic. It is the psalm most often quoted in the New Testament. Jesus quoted it (Matt. 22:44). The author of Hebrews made use of it (Heb. 1:13; 5:6; 7:17; 8:1; 10:12-13). See further references in Acts 2:34; 1 Peter 3:22; 1 Corinthians 15:25; Colossians 3:1. Jesus is both our priest and king—David's true descendant.

The point of the psalm is that God gives the king authority to rule and sustains him as long as he is just and obedient to divine law.

What has this psalm to say to modern rulers and governments? All authority to govern is still derived from God. This is an awesome responsibility. It calls for obedience to moral law and justice.

Psalm 111: "With My Whole Heart"

We have here a personal hymn of praise to God—for who he is and what he does. It is in the form of an acrostic. Each of its twenty-two lines begins with a different letter of the Hebrew alphabet.

God's Mighty Works (111:1-9)

God's mighty works are spelled out after a call to praise (v. 1):

• His wonderful and great works (vv. 2-4).
• His generous provision of food and his steadfast remembrance of the covenant relationship (v. 5).

- His providential protection of his people (v. 6).
- His moral law established (vv. 7-8).
- His redemption of his people reveals his name (or character) to be holy and awe-inspiring (v. 9). Thus the psalmist celebrated the greatness of God.

The Golden Text (111:10)

This verse may sound strange to modern ears: "The fear of the Lord is the beginning of wisdom." The word *fear* here means both *awe* and *joy* in the person and works of God. We fear to displease him. It is not cringing anxiety but reverence for our loving Father. It is the opposite of that familiarity which breeds contempt (see Ps. 53:1).

"The fear of the Lord" is descriptive of Old Testament religion in the same way that "God is love" represents the heart of New Testament faith.

Psalm 112: "Light in the Darkness"

In this wisdom psalm the fate of the righteous man (see Psalm 1) is contrasted with that of the wicked. It is an acrostic like Psalm 111, which suggests that the two poems had a common author.

A Beatitude (112:1)

The psalm begins with a blessing on the man who fears the Lord. Recall verse 10 in Psalm 111: "The fear of the Lord is the beginning of wisdom." Such a person holds God in reverence and delights to obey his commandments.

The Righteous Man's Reward (112:2-9)

He will be blessed in his *posterity*. His children will be influential in the land (v. 2). Descendants are a form of immortality in the Old Testament.

The godly person will also enjoy *prosperity*, "wealth and riches" (v. 3). Material prosperity was considered a sign of divine favor by the Hebrews. We still have similar feelings about prosperity and ask "why?" when we experience adversity.

God is gracious to the upright. "Light rises in the darkness" for the godly (v. 4). People of faith tend to look on the bright side and be optimistic. They see beyond surface appearances.

As a response to God's blessings the righteous man is *generous* in his gifts to the poor (v. 9) and in making loans to those in need (v. 5). There is a contrast between this man and Polonius in *Hamlet* who advised his son, Laertes, "Neither a borrower, nor a lender be" (I, iii).

The righteous man is *secure*. He does not live in constant fear of bad news. "His heart is firm, trusting in the Lord" (v. 7). He lives not in fear but by faith (v. 8). Therefore, his strength and power (horn) endure (v. 9*b*). The poet gives us an attractive description of the salt-of-the-earth kind of person. Note that the description is devoid of any hope of a future life beyond the grave. At best, the man would live on in the lives of his children, as far as the psalmist knew.

The Wicked Man's Punishment (112:10)

He is angry and resentful at the prosperity and security of the godly man. He "gnashes his teeth" in frustration and "melts away"—amounts to nothing. The wicked man's ambition and desire "comes to nought." His fury is self-consuming.

Note the contrast between generosity and resentment, the security of faith and the vanity of nonfaith. To see a New Testament description of the wicked man, read Luke 12:13-21. He had wealth but was not rich toward God.

The poem reflects no view of reward or punishment hereafter. How does one become righteous? (Job 25:4). Paul taught that we are justified by faith (Rom. 5:1). Those who trust in the Lord do have an integrity and stability which is real and which is not common to all.

Psalm 113: God of Majesty and Compassion

Psalms 113—114 were sung before the Passover meal, and Psalms 115—118 were sung afterward. This would have been what Jesus and his disciples sang at the Last Supper (Matt. 26:30). This psalm is a hymn of praise to the Lord. Here God's exalted majesty and his concern for outcast humanity is combined in an important lesson.

"Blessed Be the Name" (113:1-3)

The worship leader called on the congregation, "servants of the Lord," to praise the Lord. Three times in as many verses he mentioned "the name of the Lord." God's name stands for his revealed character.

Remember that in the Lord's Prayer we pray for his name to be held holy ("hallowed").

The praise of God is to go on for all eternity, "from this time forth and for evermore!" (v. 2). The praise of God is to be universal among all men, "from the rising of the sun to its setting" (v. 3).

The Majestic God Is Concerned for the Lowly (113:4-9)

God is highly exalted "above all nations." His glory is also "above the heavens" (v. 4). There is no one in all the universe who can compare with him (v. 5).

This Lord God Almighty is aware of the plight of the poor (v. 7). He lifts them from the dust and poverty, giving them dignity—he makes them "sit with princes" (v. 8). The needy live on garbage thrown on the city dump (v. 7), but God cares for them. Note Mary's song, the Magnificat in Luke 1:48. The ash heap here reminds us of Job and his plight.

In ancient times it was considered a disgrace for a married woman to be childless. Now we know that infertility may equally be due to the male. God was aware of her shame and would make her "the joyous mother of children" (v. 9). Recall the story of Hannah in 1 Samuel 2:8.

This splendid hymn of praise teaches that the God of glory cares about the underprivileged, poor, and outcast. He also acts on their behalf. We have been slow to learn this important lesson. We still tend to think of riches as a sign of divine favor and poverty as an indication of laziness or a sinful life. There are too many exceptions to make such a thesis valid. Remember the psalmist's lesson: Almighty God cares for the lowly and oppressed.

Psalm 114: "Tremble . . . at the Presence of the Lord"

As Psalm 113 is praise, so Psalm 114 celebrates the history of God's mighty acts on Israel's behalf. The Exodus from Egypt was to the Hebrews what Easter is to Christians. Both represent deliverance—from slavery and from sin.

The Exodus event was the hinge in Israel's history. Indeed, it made the nation of Israel a reality. This psalm may have been written for the Passover celebration.

The miracles of the Exodus are recounted:
• "Israel went forth from Egypt," a foreign land and bondage (v. 1).

- They dwelt safely and were self-governing in Judah and Israel, the Southern and Northern Kingdoms (v. 2).
- The sea was rolled away at the beginning of their journey, and the Jordan River was parted at journey's end (v. 3).
- God provided water from the rock during their wilderness wanderings (v. 8).

In verses 4-6 we have ecstatic poetry. The mountains and hills shared the people's joy (vv. 4,6). The sea and river were reversed, acting contrary to nature (v. 5).

The poem's climax is found in verse 7: "Tremble, O earth, at the presence of the Lord." God has been historically present with his people in times past. That is an indisputable fact. God still comes to his own; he is still at work in persons and in events. He is Lord of both nature and history. What does this mean to you?

Psalm 115: Glory to His Name

This psalm and the next two were probably sung by Jesus and his disciples after the Last Supper (Mark 14:26). They were an appropriate prelude to Gethsemane and Calvary. This psalm also gives a vivid contrast between the living God and man-made idols (vv. 3-8).

Glory Belongs to God (115:1)

We are not the ones who deserve glory. It should be given to the name of God. He is faithful and trustworthy. His love is always dependable.

The Mockery of Pagan Neighbors (115:2-8)

Israel's neighboring nations looked at her misfortune and asked, "Where is their God?" Such mockery was hard to take (see Ps. 79:10).

The poet answered with humor and ridicule similar to that used in Isaiah 41; 44. The God of heaven is sovereign—"he does whatever he pleases" (v. 3). By contrast, the idols of their pagan neighbors are helpless. They are man-made gods. (We still have lots of those.) Their helplessness is evident in that their eyes cannot see; their mouths cannot speak. They cannot hear, smell, or help. Note the biting ridicule of verse 8: "Those who make them [idols] are like them" —helpless!

A Call to Trust (115:9-18)

Three groups were invited to "trust in the Lord." These included the nation of Israel, the priests, and "you who fear the Lord" (v. 11). This latter group was perhaps the devoutly religious. God has not forgotten his own (v. 12). His blessings are bestowed on "both small and great" (v. 13). God is no respecter of persons.

The poet declared that the heavens belong to God, and the earth has been entrusted to mankind as a stewardship (v. 16). As far as he knew only the living praise God (v. 17). The psalm is concluded with the people's vow to praise the Lord "for evermore" (v. 18).

The principal point made by this psalm is the vivid contrast between God and the gods people make for themselves.

Psalm 116: "The Cup of Salvation"

Here we have the personal testimony of one who was seriously ill and almost died. The Lord heard his prayer and delivered him. He praised God and paid his vows by bringing a sacrifice. This is a moving poem of thanksgiving in the setting of worship in the Temple.

The Psalmist's Distress (116:1-11)

He began by professing his love for the Lord, who answered his prayers (vv. 1-2). He suffered the pangs of death. In agony he prayed that his life might be spared (v. 4).

God is gracious to the simple (those without guile). He delivered the poet's "soul from death . . . eyes from tears . . . and feet from stumbling." What lovely poetry! Once healed, he walked "before the Lord in the land of the living" (v. 9).

The psalmist kept his faith in God, but was sorely disappointed in the attitudes of the people around him (vv. 10-11).

The Psalmist's Declaration of Praise (116:12-19)

Note the beautiful rhetorical question in verse 12: "What shall I render to the Lord for all his bounty to me?" The answer is obviously: "Nothing is adequate." He offered his worship.

"I will lift up the cup of salvation and call on the name of the Lord" was his response (v. 13). It was a drink offering. His worship would show his gratitude. The Jews later saw "the cup of salvation" as the Passover cup. Christians have long connected the phrase with the cup of the Lord's Supper, symbolic of our salvation by Christ's blood. The "cup of salvation" is seen as a contrast to the cup of God's wrath or Jesus' suffering (recall the scene in Gethsemane).

The death of God's own is "precious" in his sight (v. 15). It is no light matter, for it represents the saints' victory and their going home.

The psalmist promised to: 1. Offer "the sacrifice of thanksgiving." 2. "Call on the name of the Lord" in praise and gratitude. 3. "Pay my vows to the Lord" or to keep his promises. He concluded with the exclamation: "Praise the Lord!" (v. 19).

This psalm shows that God continues to hear and answer our prayers. It also recognizes that there is no way in which we can adequately repay God for all his love and provision. Like the psalmist, we can show our gratitude by loving and praising the Lord.

Psalm 117: Praise the Lord, All Nations

This is the shortest psalm in the Psalter. It summoned all nations and people to praise the Lord for God's deliverance and his divine purpose—their salvation. This burst of praise celebrated the eternal mercies of God. It is a brief but powerful call to worship, with a missionary thrust.

Psalm 118: A Processional of Praise

This was Martin Luther's favorite psalm. It contains a number of memorable verses which are quoted in the New Testament. It was probably sung by the king in a procession of worshipers going up to worship at the Temple. The setting for its use appears to have been the autumn Feast of Tabernacles.

A Litany of Praise (118:1-4)

Three groups of worshipers were called on to respond: "His steadfast love endures forever." They included all Israel (v. 2), the priests (v. 3), and the devout (v. 4).

The King Declares Israel's Faith (118:5-20)

Speaking on behalf of the people, the Davidic king declared that God had heard his distress call and answered him (v. 5). With God at his side there was nothing to ultimately fear (v. 6). Israel's refuge was in the Lord (v. 8). The nation's enemies surrounded them "like bees," but God enabled the king to "cut them off" (vv. 10-12). The Lord was the source of salvation (v. 14). He gave the victory (v. 16).

At verse 19, the procession had reached the city gates of Jerusalem. The king commanded them to open, allowing the worshipers to enter and "give thanks to the Lord." The city gate was called "the gate of the Lord" because it admitted the faithful to his presence on earth within the holy of holies of the Temple.

Praise in the House of the Lord (118:21-29)

God made the disciplined remnant of Israel "the chief corner stone" (v. 22). Jesus applied these verses to himself (Mark 12:10-11). Within the Temple courtyard the priests blessed the worshipers (v. 26). This verse was quoted by the crowd when Jesus entered Jerusalem on Palm Sunday in triumph (Matt. 21:9). God is the source of light or spiritual truth and understanding (v. 27). The concluding verses are a jubilant statement of thanksgiving and praise to the Lord.

Psalm 118 Quoted in the New Testament

Look again at three significant quotations from this psalm in the New Testament:

1. As the king rode into the city the priests sang, "Blessed be he who enters in the name of the Lord!" (v. 26). This verse was chanted by the people who welcomed Jesus, the Prince of peace, to Jerusalem at the beginning of Holy Week (Mark 11:9).

2. Jesus applied the song of the rejected stone to himself at the close of the parable of the vineyard keepers (vv. 22-23; Mark 12:10-11).

3. "The Lord is God, and he has given us light" (v. 27). Jesus used the verse in his saying, "I am the light of the world" (John 8:12).

Psalm 119: A Celebration of the Law

Each verse in this longest psalm is built around a different word which is a synonym for the word of God. The word *law* occurs twenty-five times; *word* appears twenty-three times; *statutes* and *commandments* are used twenty-two times each; *surety, appointment,* and *faithfulness* are used once. The basic theme of the psalm is the law of God. The psalm rhymes in the original Hebrew, and it is an acrostic.

The poet sang the praise of the law under all kinds of circumstances:

persecution, false accusation, temptation, and intellectual doubt. Psalm 19:7-10 is restated in Psalm 119.

The law is not a substitute for God but a guide to doing his will. It is not a burden to the psalmist but a joy. The law enables the poet to live in communion with God. The "statutes" represent the written law of God. The "word" is a dynamic communication of God's will for mankind. Sometimes the law is also presented as "promise."

The point of the psalm is that obedience to God's law is the way to happiness. The poet asked divine help in understanding and keeping the law (vv. 1-8). God's word in one's heart brings joy and protects the believer from sin (vv. 9-16). The poet prayed for deliverance from his enemies (vv. 25-32). He declared his loyalty to God's law (vv. 33-40). He prayed that he might understand the law more fully (vv. 41-48). He asked that he might be able to answer his foes who taunted him (vv. 49-56).

The psalmist kept his confidence even in times of persecution (vv. 57-64). He declared his devotion to the Lord (vv. 65-72) and recognized that we can learn from what we suffer (vv. 73-80). God's ways are just (vv. 81-88). The psalmist prayed again to be delivered from his enemies (vv. 89-96). He had an unshakable faith in the word of God (vv. 97-104).

The poet found the law to be sweet and beautiful (vv. 105-112). He prayed for divine help (vv. 113-120), praying for the Lord's intervention on his behalf (vv. 121-128). He affirmed his loyalty to the law (vv. 129-136). He praised the justice and righteousness of God's law (vv. 137-152).

The psalmist cried out to be saved from persecution (vv. 153-160) and asked that his life might be spared (vv. 161-168). He declared his own faith and devotion (vv. 169-176). He promised to sing God's praise in gratitude for divine deliverance.

Psalm 119 is the Old Testament's greatest expression of love for God's law. The psalmist meditated upon the law, loved it, and delighted in it. Still, it is something to be obeyed. The law is not static but dynamic. It provides light and guidance. Obeying the law establishes fellowship with the living God. The psalm's meaning is clearly apparent to those who read it thoughtfully.

The poet concluded the psalm with a petition for understanding. He recommitted himself to obey the law and confessed his reliance on the Shepherd's care (vv. 169-176). This is formal Hebrew wisdom poetry. While the psalm is repetitious, it is always true to its theme: the celebration of God's law.

Psalm 120: The Deceitful Tongue

This is one of the pilgrim psalms (Pss. 120—134). It is a kind of folk song by one who lived far from Jerusalem and his native land. Note the title on these psalms is "A Song of Ascents." They were sung by pilgrims as they went up to Jerusalem to observe the great worship festivals.

"Deliver Me" (120:1-2)

The psalmist was in great distress and cried out to the Lord. His prayer is set in quotation marks in verse 2. He wanted to be delivered from persons of "lying lips" and a "deceitful tongue."

A Curse on His Enemies (120:3-4)

He prayed that they might receive retribution appropriate to their offense. His enemies shot arrows of falsehood trying to destroy his reputation—so he asked that they be destroyed by "warrior's sharp arrows." By their deceit they had kindled the fire of enmity against the psalmist. He prayed that they would be consumed by the hot coals of the broom tree. Like heart pine, the wood of the broom tree produced an especially hot and long-burning fire.

"Woe Is Me" (120:5-7)

The psalmist lived in a foreign land among warlike people (v. 6). The nomads of Kedar lived in the desert south of Damascus (Isa. 21:13,16-17). Meshech was an area in northern Asia Minor where the people traded in bronze vessels and slaves (Ezek. 32:26-27). The poet's references to the tongue are similar to the Epistle of James.

Psalm 121: Where Do We Go for Help?

This favorite psalm shows us God on guard. It beautifully pictures divine care and protection. It answers the question, Where can we go for help?

Psalm 121 was doubtless sung around the campfires of pilgrims en route to Jerusalem and its Temple.

"I Will Lift Up My Eyes" (121:1-2)

In the time of crisis, if we look around us we feel threatened. If we look within our own hearts, we are afraid. It is only when we look up to the hills and the One who made them that we feel secure.

There is something special about the hills. Artists and poets have long
felt their attraction. The psalmist looked beyond the hills on which Jerusalem was built to "the Lord who made heaven and earth." A pilgrim
asked the question in verse 1, and a worship leader gave the reply in
verses 2-8.

God on Guard (121:3-8)

The Lord is said to keep or protect the pilgrim six times in these verses.
He does not let our foot slip on dangerous mountain paths (v. 3). Sentries
may fall asleep at their posts, but not the Lord. He watches over Israel
continuously, never dozing (vv. 3-4).

God protects his own from sunstroke. He is our shade (v. 5). He also
keeps us safe from moonstroke, thought by the ancients to be harmful.
The word *lunatic* used to describe the insane came from this belief. Day
and night God keeps us safe (v. 6).

God will keep us from all evil (v. 7). Recall the petition in the Lord's
Prayer, "deliver us from evil." He preserves our life. God watched over
the pilgrims going up to Jerusalem and returning home. He protects us in
our daily work, and we can trust him for the future, "for evermore" (v.
8).

As incredible as it seems, the God who made heaven and earth cares
about us. His love and protection are ours. That is the theme of this eloquent poem.

There are many hills and mountains in the Bible. But none towers
higher than Calvary, where heaven and earth met and we found our
help.

Psalm 122: Pray for Peace

This psalm is a pilgrim's prayer for the peace of Jerusalem, the Holy
City. We believe that peace and justice follow the establishment of the
kingdom of God. This psalm is a beautiful call to worship for persons of
all time, especially in the first verse.

The Pilgrim Reaches Jerusalem (122:1-5)

The poet was glad when his friends first suggested he go with them to
Jerusalem's Temple, "the house of the Lord" (v. 1). Perhaps he was a
youth at the time. Anticipation became realization once his feet stood

"within your gates, O Jerusalem" (v. 2).

The next verses are a poetic reflection on the importance of Jerusalem in the life and faith of his people. "The tribes go up" from near and far to celebrate the presence of God in the Temple. They come to worship and "give thanks to the name of the Lord" (v. 4). The city was also the seat of the Davidic throne (v. 5). It symbolized both religious and political unity.

Prayer for Jerusalem's Peace (122:6-9)

Peace (*shalom* in Hebrew) means more than the absence of strife. It also stands for health, wholeness, and well-being. "Salem" in the word *Jerusalem* means peace. The psalmist prayed that the city might prosper and enjoy security from its enemies (v. 7). "Peace be within you!" (v. 8). The poet wished Jerusalem well because it contained "the house of the Lord our God" (v. 9).

Jesus may have had this psalm in mind when he wept over Jerusalem and said, "Would that even today you knew the things that make for peace!" (Luke 19:42).

Psalm 123: Look to the Lord

The first verse is in the first person singular. It was sung by a priest. The rest of the psalm is in the first person plural and would have been sung by the worshipers.

The psalmist lifted his eyes to God "enthroned in the heavens" (v. 1). This is similar to the opening phrase of the Lord's Prayer. To say that God is transcendent means that he has power to help us.

As slaves look to their master, "so our eyes look to the Lord our God" to receive mercy (v. 2). He is the merciful king of the universe (see Isa. 30:18).

The poet pled for divine grace: "Have mercy upon us, O Lord" (v. 3). His enemies were contemptuous and scornful.

Psalm 124: The Lord on Our Side

This psalm is a thanksgiving for national deliverance. God is given credit for the victory. Had it not been for his divine intervention the people of Israel would have been "swallowed . . . up alive" and consumed by the fiery anger of their enemies (v. 3). In the following verse their potential destruction is described in terms of "the flood . . . torrent . . . [and] raging waters" (vv. 4-5).

Israel blessed the Lord for not allowing them to fall prey to their enemies (v. 6). The nation must have been in real danger. The psalmist described their deliverance as a bird escaping from the fowler's snare (v. 7).

The final verse is a word of praise: "Our help is in the name of the Lord, who made heaven and earth." (See Pss. 32:6; 69:1-2,14-15; 121:2.)

Psalm 125: God's Protection Surrounds Us

Most affirmations of faith in the Psalms are personal. This one is on behalf of the nation. The psalm is a prayer in praise of God's protection. It expresses confidence and asks for divine help.

"Those Who Trust in the Lord" (125:1-3)

Those who trust in the Lord" (v. 1) are secure. As the mountains surround Jerusalem, "so the Lord is round about his people" perpetually (v. 2). Zion is the mountain on which the Temple was built. The last Jewish Temple there was destroyed by the Roman general Titus in AD 70. Today it is the site of a mosque called the Dome of the Rock.

God's presence is his people's protection. The poet expressed his faith that foreign rule of the Holy Land would not last for long. "The scepter of wickedness" would not long endure in "the land allotted to the righteous" (v. 3). Otherwise, the righteous might be tempted to despair.

"Do Good, O Lord" (125:4-5)

The psalmist prayed that God would bless "those who are upright in their hearts" (v. 4). They are the faithful remnant of Israel. He asked that those who are crooked or perverse may be "led away" by the Lord.

The final line in the psalm is a prayer: "Peace be in Israel!" (v. 5).

Psalm 126: The Lord Has Done Great Things

Psalm 85 is similar to this psalm, recalling past divine intervention and praying for renewal. The first three verses remember the joy of those who returned from Exile in Babylon. However, their return was followed by a time of hardship and bitter disappointment. It paralleled, in some sense, the Reconstruction period in the southern states following the American Civil War. The Hebrew poet prayed for the renewal of God's favor and for prosperity to be restored.

Gratitude for What the Lord Did (126:1-3)

God had "restored the fortunes of Zion" when he brought them back from captivity in Babylon. It was like a dream come true (v. 1). Laughter and shouts of joy expressed their happiness at answered prayer. Even other nations took note of the great things the Lord did for his people (v. 2). Israel was truly glad at his grace (v. 3).

A Prayer for Future Renewal (126:4-6)

The poet prayed that God might restore their fortunes again, "like the watercourses in the Negeb!" (v. 4). The Negeb is the desert to the south of Judah—with its dry riverbeds which were filled after the winter rains. Verse 5 is a lovely prayer, "May those who sow in tears reap with shouts of joy!" The final verse is an oracle promising that it shall be so. God will grant their request.

We can endure present hardships in the hope of better times. Even in our suffering there is an opportunity to witness to God's grace.

Psalm 127: Depend on the Lord

All human effort which lacks the Lord's blessing comes to nothing. That is the theme of this short psalm. It is an example of Wisdom Literature attributed to the wise King Solomon (note the title).

On Building a House (127:1-2)

The "house" in verse 1 may refer to a dwelling or to the Temple, the house of God. He is the ultimate builder as he is the city's ultimate Watchman. Hard work and anxious toil alone will not get the job done. What is required is a combination of human effort and divine blessing: work as though all depends on us, and pray as if all depends on God. That is an unbeatable combination. The psalmist reminds us that we are dependent on God. (See Matt. 6:25-34.)

A reassuring word is given the insomniac: "he gives to his beloved sleep" (v. 2).

On Building a Home (127:3-5)

Sons were regarded as a special blessing in ancient times. A man who has sons while he is still young is especially fortunate—they give him an advantage like sharp "arrows in the hand of a warrior. . . . Happy is the man who has his quiver full of them!" (vv. 4-5). His sons will be his protection in court (at the city gate).

God is the ultimate builder of both houses and homes. He builds, watches, and gives his protection. This psalm calls on us to acknowledge our dependence on him.

Psalm 128: The Blessings of Reverence

The God-fearing man is the subject of this psalm (v. 1). Psalms 127 and 128 focus on the Hebrew family. Both are considered Wisdom Literature, the product of an Israelite sage.

The Reverent Man (128:1-2)

This psalm sounds like a commentary on Psalm 111:10, "The fear of the Lord is the beginning of wisdom." The person who has reverence for God lives a life of respect and right conduct; he "walks in his ways" (v. 1).

As a reward he will "eat the fruit of the labor of [his] hands." The reverent person will be blessed materially. He will also be happy and at peace; "it shall be well with you" (v. 2).

The Godly Man's Family (128:3-4)

His wife will be as fruitful as a vine—a sign of divine favor to the Hebrews. His children will be "like olive shoots around your table." The olive tree is an evergreen, a symbol of vitality. The young shoots grow from the trunk of the tree. The man who fears the Lord is blessed materially, spiritually, and in terms of his growing family.

A Benediction (128:5-6)

Perhaps a priest pronounced the conclusion of the psalms: May the Lord bless you from his Temple on Mount Zion, his dwelling place on earth. May you see Jerusalem prosper all your life, and may you live to "see your children's children!" Old age was considered a blessing and a sign of divine favor.

The final word: "Peace be upon Israel!" (v. 6).

With eloquent simplicity the psalmist reminds us of life's basic values: meaningful work to do, a happy marriage, the blessing of children, and a right relationship with our Creator. Such values should be as cherished today as in the poet's time.

Psalm 129: The Enemies of Zion

Israel's enemies had been a problem to the nation, as this lament indicates. Still, the Lord had preserved her. This psalm is similar to Psalm 124 in thought and style.

Persecuted but Preserved (129:1-4)

Despite all that Israel had suffered at the hands of her enemies, God had kept her. The young nation came out of Egypt (see Hos. 11:1). Many tried to destroy the Israelites: the Egyptians, Canaanites, Philistines, Assyrians, and Babylonians. One day the Romans would succeed (in AD 70).

The poet described the suffering of Israel at the hands of her enemies as being plowed with long furrows. But God kept his people despite their persecution at the hands of multiple foes (v. 4).

A Curse on Their Enemies (129:5-8)

"May all who hate Zion be put to shame," the psalmist prayed (v. 5). He asked that they wither like shallow rooted grass which grows on the flat roof (v. 6), never producing useful hay or grain (v. 7).

Israel's enemies will never enjoy "the blessing of the Lord" (v. 8). The people of God persevere and will know no ultimate destruction (see Matt. 16:18). Israel considered their enemies to be the Lord's enemies, as well. This is a very human psalm.

Psalm 130: "Out of the Depths"

In historic Christian usage this is one of the seven penitential psalms (or psalms of repentance; see also Pss. 6; 32; 38; 51; 102; 143). It comes from the psalmist's dark distress and sounds the notes of hope and forgiveness.

"Out of the Depths" (130:1-2)

The poet's distress stemmed from his sin and alienation from God. His problem was guilt, and his need was for forgiveness. He cried from the depths of despair like a drowning man. He pled that God would hear and answer his "supplications."

God of Grace (130:3-4)

Having confessed his need and entered a plea for pardon, the poet next magnified God's graciousness. If God gave us what we deserved, "who could stand?" (see Gal. 2:16 and Rom. 3:20). But God forgives (see 86:5), and this inspires our reverence and gratitude (v. 4). "Fear" in this verse means obedience and devotion, which is inspired by divine forgiveness. Jesus taught that those who have been forgiven much, love much.

Waiting for the Lord (130:5-6)

In great expectation the poet waited for the word of divine pardon. That was his hope and his salvation. He was as anxious to hear the word of the Lord as the weary night watchman is to see the dawn.

The Nation's Hope (130:7-8)

Salvation is corporate as well as individual. God was concerned with the salvation of the nation of Israel as well as individuals within it. He will save the church as a whole as well as members of it. While salvation is personal, it is not selfish. Salvation is a family affair—it involves the family of God, the church made up of all born-again believers.

Only God can redeem his people from their sins (Mark 10:45). Israel's hope was in the Lord (v. 7). His love is dependable and his forgiveness adequate.

Psalm 131: Submission to God's Will

The psalmist learned to live within his capabilities and to be content with his lot in life. His attitude is much like that of Paul in Philippians. This psalm of trust takes the form of a personal testimony. Once he had been proud and haughty; then he came to have a more realistic self-appraisal (v. 1).

The poet is at peace with himself. That is remarkable, for many people are "walking civil wars" because they have such low self-esteem or unrealistic ambitions. His soul is as calm as a quieted child secure at its mother's breast (v. 2). The mental picture is something like a beautiful madonna holding the infant Jesus. It is a portrayal of genuine humility and trust which leads to security.

The third verse is a call for Israel to "hope in the Lord." It may have been added to the psalm for use in congregational worship. John Greenleaf Whittier's poem is in this vein:

Drop Thy still dews of quietness,
  Till all our strivings cease;
Take from our souls the strain and stress,
  And let our ordered lives confess
The beauty of Thy peace.

Psalm 132: David and the Lord

This is a royal psalm written prior to the Exile in Babylon. It focuses on the ark of the covenant and King David's desire to build a Temple to house it (see 2 Sam. 7.)

King David's Desire (132:1-5)

The Lord was reminded of the hardships David had endured in his desire to build a sanctuary for the ark of the covenant (see 1 Chron. 22:14). He vowed to transfer the ark to Jerusalem (vv. 3-5) and to establish "a dwelling place for the Mighty One of Jacob" (see 2 Sam. 7:1-2). The poet asked that David's determination be remembered, not only for his sake but also for the favor of succeeding Davidic kings (see v. 10).

Reenacting the Ark's Removal (132:6-10)

There must have been a dramatic processional in which the transfer of the ark to Jerusalem was reenacted by worshipers. David had heard of the ark while in his hometown of Bethlehem, called Ephrathah here (v. 6). He located it in the fields of Jaar, a poetic abbreviation of Kiriath-jearim (see 2 Sam. 6:2-12).

Notice the quotation marks in verse 7. The choir called on other worshipers to go up to Jerusalem and worship "at his footstool" (the ark which represented the Lord's dwelling place on earth).

God Chose David and Zion (132:11-18)

This portion of the psalm contains two oracles. The first is God's promise to David (vv. 11-12; 2 Sam. 7:2-17). God said he would put one of David's sons on the throne after him (v. 11). However, the promise was conditional on the son's obedience to the law and covenant (v. 12). This promise reached its fulfillment in Christ, who was obedient unto death.

The second oracle tells how God chose Zion or Jerusalem as "his habitation" (v. 13). The Lord promised to dwell there and to "abundantly bless" the city. Her poor would be provided bread (v. 15). Jerusalem's priests would be clothed with salvation, and its "saints" (the devout believers—see 30:4) would "shout for joy" (v. 16).

The power of David (horn) would be great, and his lamp would not go out (v. 17). The king was promised that his enemies would be defeated and that his own crown would not lose its luster (v. 18). Such promises were transferred in Christian thought from David and Zion to Christ and the church. God is present today in his Son and in his body of believers.

Psalm 133: "Dwell in Unity"

This wisdom psalm focuses on family unity—peace among brothers. There is often rivalry between brothers, both blood brothers and spiritual brothers. We seem to delight in fighting among ourselves, much to our discredit.

The poet said that unity among brethren is like the fragrant oil used to anoint Aaronic priests at their ordination. It flowed like perfume from their head down onto the candidate's full beard. Unity is like the refreshing and life-giving dew on Mount Hermon, the most prominent mountain to the north of the Promised Land. Often snowcapped, it is in view from much of Galilee on a clear day.

Unity in Zion and within the family of God is a blessing, "life for evermore" (v. 3). In the New Testament this fellowship between fellow believers, brethren, is called *koinonia* or Christian fellowship. Such unity is precious and too rare, in the psalmist's day and in our own. Recall Jesus' high priestly prayer in John 17.

Psalm 134: A Psalm of Blessing

This is the last of the psalms of ascent to Jerusalem (Pss. 120—134). The first two verses are a hymn calling on worshipers to "bless the Lord." The third verse is a prayer (probably by the priests) that God would bless the people.

"Bless the Lord" (134:1-2)

This is an invitation calling for the "servants of the Lord" to worship and "bless the Lord." Night services were held in the Temple during the autumn Feast of Tabernacles (v. 1). Lifting one's hands was the attitude of prayer among the Jews (see Ps. 28:2; 1 Tim. 2:8).

We bless God by expressing our adoration and praise of him in worship.

"The Lord Bless You" (134:3)

This is a benediction which asks that the Lord might bless the worshipers "from Zion." The Lord who made heaven and earth dwelled in the holy of holies. God's blessings are both particular and universal.

Psalm 135: A Hymn of Praise to God

We have here a hymn of praise to God as the Lord of both creation and history. Scholars think that it dates from a time after the Exile in Babylon. It is a combination of other psalms and Old Testament passages skillfully woven together.

"Praise the Lord" (135:1-4)

This is a call to worship and praise. It is directed to the priests and worshipers who stand "in the courts of the house of our God!" (v. 2). His name is to be praised because "the Lord is good" (v. 3) and because by his grace he chose Israel for his own people (v. 4).

Why We Praise the Lord (135:5-18)

The reasons for man's praise of God are spelled out.

1. He is Lord of creation (vv. 5-7). God is mighty, and he is sovereign "in heaven and on earth" (v. 6). He controls nature: the clouds and lightning, wind and rain (v. 7).

2. God was Lord of Hebrew history, the Exodus from Egypt, and the conquest of Canaan (vv. 8-12). He "smote the first-born of Egypt" (v. 8). By many "signs and wonders" the Lord brought his people out of captivity (v. 9). He gave them victories over their enemies in Transjordan (Sihon and Og) and over the tribes who occupied the Land of Promise (v. 11). The Lord gave the land to Israel as their heritage (v. 12).

Verses 13-14 are a poetic interlude of praise to God.

3. We praise God because he is mightier than all pagan deities (vv. 15-18). Their idols were man-made (v. 15). They were impotent and powerless to help their devotees (vv. 16-17). Men are no better than the gods they serve (v. 18).

Concluding Summons to Praise (135:19-21)

This call to worship is addressed to the house of Israel or the nation, to the priests ("house of Aaron," v. 19), and to their assistants (the Levites, v. 20). The final verse blesses the Lord, "who dwells in Jerusalem" (v. 21).

God is to be praised by mankind for both who he is and what he does. He is worthy of our worship and adoration. Praise has its points of beginning not in mankind but in God. Note that the Model Prayer, given to us by Jesus, begins with the praise of God and then proceeds to human needs. Is this the pattern of our prayers?

Psalm 136: "His Steadfast Love"

Composed in the post-Exilic period, this is a worship hymn which was used at the great festivals. It was called the Great Hallel (Praise) and is similar to Psalm 135 in content—a thanksgiving to God as Lord of creation and history. The psalm has a familiar refrain, "for his steadfast love endures forever," which is repeated in each verse. This probably indicates that it was sung antiphonally by the choir and congregation.

Call to Give Thanks (136:1-3)

The congregation was called to praise "the Lord." This is his covenant name revealed to Moses at the burning bush (Ex. 3). The poet also called him "the God of gods" and "the Lord of lords." God is the supreme Sovereign over heaven and earth.

God and Creation (136:4-9)

By his wisdom God "made the heavens" (v. 5), "spread out the earth" (v. 6), and made the sun, moon, and stars (vv. 7-9). His love is always dependable and trustworthy.

God and Israel (136:10-26)

The psalmist rehearsed God's mighty acts in the history of his people, Israel.

The first event cited was the Exodus (vv. 10-15). God struck down the firstborn of Egypt and brought the Hebrews out of bondage. He "divided the Red Sea," enabling Israel to pass through it in safety—then overthrew Pharaoh's army in the sea.

God "led his people through the wilderness" wanderings (v. 16).

The Lord also led them in the conquest of Canaan (vv. 17-22). By his help mighty kings were defeated, and Israel received the land "as a heritage" (v. 21).

We have a recapitulation of the mighty acts of God on behalf of his people in verses 23-25. God "remembered us in our low estate . . . and rescued us from our foes." A splendid line occurs in verse 25: "He . . . gives food to all flesh" or "to all his creatures" (NEB). This speaks of God's universal providence. He not only made everything and everyone, but he also sustains and provides for us all. This is the basis of stewardship—God's prior claim.

The final verse is a summons to thanksgiving: "O give thanks to the God of heaven, for his steadfast love endures for ever." This is the only place in the Psalms in which the Almighty is called "the God of heaven."

God's providence in the past gives us confidence to trust him today and to hope for the future. The theme of this psalm is God's unchanging love to his people. He is our Creator, Provider, and Deliverer. These terms reflect the doctrines of creation, providence, and salvation.

Psalm 137: Homesick

This highly emotional psalm is both beautiful and horrible. It reflects love of Jerusalem and hatred for the city's enemies. Its keynote is grief and not simply anger. The historical setting of the psalm was the conquest of Jerusalem in 586 BC. The Babylonians carried off the most skilled and intelligent Judeans into exile. These people felt literally cut off from God, whom they thought dwelled in their Holy City, Jerusalem. The poem reflects religious homesickness. The poet must have been a victim of the Exile himself—numbered among those in the foreign land.

"By the Waters of Babylon" (137:1-6)

The psalmist found himself living along the Tigris and Euphrates Rivers in Babylon. He had carried his stringed instrument with him into Exile. "We sat down and wept" (v. 1). That was the posture of mourners in the ancient Near East. They would sit in the dust. The captives remembered Zion (the city of Jerusalem with its Temple) and hung their harps on the willow trees which grew along the river banks (v. 2). In a few words, the poet pictured the sad scene.

Insult was added to grief when their captors tormented them with a demand for music and mirth (v. 3). Perhaps the Babylonians would have found the Jewish Temple music quaint and amusing. However, the psalmist felt it would be traitorous to "sing the Lord's song in a foreign land" (v. 4).

The psalmist pronounced a curse on himself if he should ever forget Jerusalem, his spiritual home. The results of the curse sound like those of a stroke victim: may his right hand, with which he played, be paralyzed and wither away; may his tongue cleave to the roof of his mouth, leaving him unable to speak or sing. He would not be a traitor to Jerusalem!

This passage could mean that the poet thought of the Lord as a local deity, whose presence was limited to Jerusalem, while the Judeans were in far-off Babylon. We must not try to limit God to the places where he has been real in our own experience. He is the Lord of all places and of all people.

A Curse on the Enemies of God (137:7-9)

The psalmist prayed that the Lord would remember the treachery of their neighbors, the Edomites. They were the blood brothers of the Judeans—descendents of Esau, the brother of Jacob. The Edomites had gloated when Jerusalem fell, saying, "Down with it, down with it, down to its very foundations!" (v. 7, NEB; see Joel 3:19 and Jer. 49:7-22). Enmity between Jews and Arabs is centuries old.

"Babylon, the destroyer" was also cursed by the psalmist (see v. 8). He cursed them by pronouncing a blessing on whoever conquered Babylon and repaid them for their cruelty. Those were crude and cruel times—like the twentieth century! The poet not only longed for Jerusalem; he also longed for retaliation on his enemies, whom he considered the Lord's enemies, as well. The prayer of verse 9 is unspeakably cruel. He asked for genocide, the annihilation of a race of people.

What are we as modern Christians to make of this psalm?

• It reminds us of the depravity of human nature, including our own. Never forget that the holocaust occurred in modern times and in a nation with many Christians.

• It reminds us of the folly of blind, irrational nationalism.

• It is clearly pre-Christian, reflecting a time when people had not yet learned that God's ways are not mankind's ways.

• It shows us how desperately we need to hear and heed the teachings of the New Testament. Jesus taught us to love our enemies (Matt. 5:38-42,44) as he did. Paul wrote that we should learn to "bless those who persecute you; bless and do not curse them" (Rom. 12:14).

• It shows the psalmist's loyalty to his faith even in a time of severe testing.

Psalm 138: A Prayer of Gratitude

The psalmist was grateful that the Lord had answered his prayers and delivered him from trouble.

"I Give Thee Thanks, O Lord" (138:1-3)

The psalmist stood in the Temple courtyard, giving thanks to God with his "whole heart" (v. 1). The "gods" in verse 1 may refer to the angels or to pagan deities. Note that *The New English Bible* omits the word, translating the verse: "boldly, O God, will I sing psalms to thee." The poet bowed toward the holy of holies and gave thanks for the Lord's steadfast love and faithfulness. God had answered his cry (v. 3).

"All the Kings of the Earth Shall Praise Thee" (138:4-8)

These verses sound much like Psalm 23. The poet affirmed his faith in God, who preserved his life in troubled times. God had a purpose for his life and had delivered him from his enemies. His final prayer was that God would not forsake him since he was the "work" of the Almighty's hands. God made him and valued him—and us.

Psalm 139: "Whither Shall I Go from Thy Spirit?"

The theme of this beautiful psalm is the presence of God. The author of the poem knew the Lord intimately. It is a powerful affirmation of faith. The psalm celebrates God's knowledge, power, and presence.

God's Unlimited Knowledge (139:1-6)

God knows us—everything we have ever thought or done, both good and bad. He knows the intentions of our hearts, our very motives, which may not even be known to us.

The poet said that God had searched him and knew him (v. 1). God knew his posture as well as his thoughts (v. 2). He was acquainted with all his ways and with all he spoke—his deeds and his words (vv. 3-4). God went before him and came behind him (v. 5). The poet concluded, "Such knowledge is too wonderful for me" (v. 6).

God's Universal Presence (139:7-12)

There may have been a time in the poet's life when he felt guilty and had tried to escape or hide from God. He learned that such is impossible—there can be no secret crimes. One cannot evade "the Hound of Heaven."

God is everyplace, the psalmist declared. He is in heaven and in Sheol, the abode of the dead (not hell). "The wings of the morning" are a poetic phrase for the spread of light at dawn. God is even at sea (v. 9). There is no running away from God any more than one can run away from oneself. No matter where we are his hand shall lead us, and his right hand shall hold us (v. 10). What a precious promise!

Even darkness does not hide us from God. The dark is like light to him (v. 12). God's presence can haunt us. It may be unwelcome and unwanted; however, there is also great security in it. He is with us, protecting us, loving us, even when we may not want him. This is an insightful section.

God Made Us and We Are His (139:13-18)

The poet marveled at God's creation in the birth process. Thoughtful persons still do. (See Job 10:8-11.)

In beautiful, poetic language God is said to have "knit" the poet together in his mother's womb (v. 13). Thus the Lord knew him from the beginning (v. 14). In verse 15 he said he was made in secret "in the depths of the earth." That may refer to the dark recesses of the womb or to the fact of our creation "from dust." That is, we are creatures.

God saw the poet as an embryo long before any person saw the evidence of his development inside his mother's body. Also, God recorded his development day by day—a fascinating process we now know!

The psalmist was stunned at the magnitude of God's thoughts. The more we learn about the human body and the natural world, the more we should stand in awe and worship. Waking or sleeping, God is there (v. 18).

God, the Universal Judge (139:19-24)

Vengeance belongs to God. He alone can judge correctly, for he knows all the circumstances and our inner motives. The wicked were considered God's enemies. The poet saw them as his own, as well (vv. 21-22).

The concluding verses 23-24 are a beautiful prayer. The poet was keenly aware of his own imperfection and of his desire to do right:

> Search me, O God, and know my heart!
> Try me and know my thoughts!

He then asked that God would "see if there be any wicked (hurtful) way in me." *The New English Bible* translates it, "any path that grieves thee." He concluded by praying, "lead me in the way everlasting" or in the ancient way (see Jer. 6:16). These verses acknowledge our dependence on God, which is at the heart of faith.

Psalm 139 is an "incomparable lyric of God's presence."[1] Historically, this psalm has been used in Christian worship at Easter (as Ps. 22 is associated with the cross). It reminds us that in his incarnation Jesus knows us, for he became what we are (human). The verse "When I awake, I am still with thee" (18) has been applied to the resurrection. The psalm celebrates God's knowledge and his creative power, as well as his moral correction.

Note

1. Erik Routley, *Exploring the Psalms* (Philadelphia: Westminster Press, 1979), p. 52.

Psalm 140: "Deliver Me, O Lord"

The psalmist prayed that God would deliver him from his enemies —and punish them.

"Deliver Me" (140:1-8)

The poet's enemies were called "evil men . . . violent . . . wicked . . . and arrogant." Their speech was sharp and poisonous (v. 3). Romans 3:13 quotes from Psalms 5:9 and 140:3.

The psalmist prayed to be delivered from and protected from such fierce enemies (vv. 1,4). They were like skilled hunters, setting a trap and a net to ensnare him (v. 5).

He prayed that God would hear his cry (v. 6) and be his "strong deliverer" (v. 7). He was also anxious that God not grant "the desires of the wicked" (v. 8).

Vindicate Me (140:9-11)

The psalmists, of course, had never heard the text, "Vengeance is mine, I will repay, says the Lord" (Rom. 12:19*b*). Therefore, they took matters into their own hands, or at least into their prayers.

The poet here was praying that the curse of his enemies might be poured out on their own heads. "Let the mischief of their lips overwhelm them! Let burning coals fall upon them! Let them be cast into pits, no more to rise!" (vv. 9-10). He asked that the hunter become the hunted (v. 11) and prayed vividly for the destruction of his enemies.

God Is Just (140:12-13)

The psalmist was convinced that God would champion the cause of the righteous who were afflicted by their enemies. He "executes justice for the needy" (v. 12).

In response, the righteous would give thanks for their deliverance. They will dwell in God's presence as they worship (v. 13). Despite the psalmist's bitterness toward his enemies, he expressed a confident faith in God.

Psalm 141: The Golden Gift of Silence

The psalmist appears to have been a young man in danger of being influenced by wicked men. But he had the presence of mind and maturity of faith to ask for God's help in resisting temptation.

Prayer as Worship (141:1-2)

The poet called on God, asking that his voice be heard (v. 1). In the second verse he pled that his prayer might be accepted as incense offered to God and that lifting his hands in prayer might be equated with offering the evening sacrifice (see Ex. 29:38-42).

The Golden Gift of Silence (141:3-4)

The psalmist was tempted to make an impression on rich but evil men by the use of his glib tongue. Perhaps he was being drawn into their lewd talk and callous attitudes which showed no regard for God or things of the Spirit. With insight he prayed, "Set a guard over my mouth, O Lord, keep watch over the door of my lips!" (v. 3).

How important it is that we learn when to be silent as well as when to speak. How much better off we would be if we didn't think we must always have the last word. Oh that we would invite God to guard our lips as the psalmist did!

He also prayed that he might not be tempted by the fancy foods and social life of the wicked (v. 4).

Overcoming Temptation (141:5-10)

It is better to be rebuked by a good man than praised by those who are evil (v. 5). The anointing with perfumed oil was a sign of courtesy shown guests at a banquet (Ps. 23:5).

The poet prayed for the destruction of evil men (v. 7). He also asked that they might not catch him in temptation's trap (v. 9), but that evil would boomerang on them (v. 10; 140:9).

The poet's prayer in this psalm is a preventive one. He recognized the attraction and peril for temptation and prayed for deliverance from it. We are not always that smart. Surely, this is a wiser prayer than yielding to temptation and then having to turn to the Lord in repentance (Ps. 51). It is better to keep temptation at bay (see Matt. 18:7-9). Prayer is an aid in resisting the tempter.

Psalm 142: "No Man Cares for Me"

The lonely and distressed poet poured out his heart before the Lord in this psalm. His great loneliness stemmed from the feeling that nobody cared whether he lived or died. He agonized in prayer.

The Poet's Complaint (142:1-4)

"Nobody knows the trouble I've seen" could have been the psalmist's theme song. He told God about his trouble (v. 2). He was confident that the Almighty knew his "way" (v. 3). A Christian can believe even more strongly that God knows our need and understands us—since the incarnation! "Who in every respect has been tempted as we are, yet without sinning" (Heb. 4:15). At the ascension Jesus carried our humanity into the Godhead. The Lord really does know what it is like to be human, to be tempted. He understands and forgives us when we repent.

The psalmist's enemies were out to trap him (v. 3*b*). He looked to his right for protection, for a friend, someone to help. But he concluded, "No man cares for me" (v. 4). He felt utterly forsaken.

The Psalmist's Refuge (142:5-7)

He had the good sense to turn to the Lord in his loneliness and despair (v. 5). He was "brought very low!" (v. 6). While his enemies were strong, he knew that God was stronger and could deliver him (v. 6). He felt imprisoned by his situation, or he may have literally been put into prison on the false accusations of his foes (v. 7).

Note that he still had faith in God—and in good men. He believed "the righteous will surround me" (v. 7). He found bright hope even in the darkness of his lament. We, too, do well not to lose heart.

Psalm 143: "No Man Living Is Righteous Before Thee"

There are seven psalms of penitence: 6, 32, 38, 51, 102, and 130. This is the last of the group. The psalmist did not claim sinless perfection. He confessed that he was a sinner—as all persons are (v. 2b). The psalm is thought to be a late one and to have been written after the Exile.

A Cry for Help (143:1-2)

The poet prayed that God would hear his prayer, not because of his faithfulness but out of God's faithfulness to his covenant with Israel. He acknowledged that he belonged to a sinful race. (See Rom. 3:20; Gal. 2:16.)

The Psalmist's Need (143:3-6)

His enemies were pursuing him. If they caught him, they would crush him and make him "sit in darkness like those long dead" (v. 3b). He was exhausted with the chase (v. 4).

The poet remembered God's mighty acts in times past. He was probably recalling God's creation of the world and his creation of the nation of Israel by the Exodus from Egypt. God's providential care in days past gives us faith for today and for tomorrow.

The author's soul thirsted for God as parched land thirsts for refreshing rain (v. 6).

The Psalmist's Petition (143:7-12)

He was in urgent need for his prayer to be answered—or perhaps impatient (v. 7). "Those who go down to the Pit" are those who die. He prayed that he might hear from the Lord "in the morning" (soon). He earnestly wanted divine guidance, as well as deliverance from his enemies: "Teach me the way I should go" (v. 8). "Let thy good spirit lead me on a level path" (v. 10).

In a final appeal the poet prayed that God would deliver him "for thy name's sake . . . in thy righteousness . . . and in thy steadfast love" (vv. 11-12). He also asked for the destruction of his enemies.

The poet made an honest appeal to God, asking for divine guidance and deliverance. He longed for the presence of God in his life, as well as to be rescued.

Psalm 144: Victory and Prosperity

We have a combination of two types of psalms here. The first half is a royal psalm (vv. 1-11). The second portion is wisdom poetry (vv. 12-15). It may have been used as a coronation song.

A Royal Prayer (144:1-11)

This is obviously the prayer of a soldier, a warrior-king. He credited God with teaching him the skills of warfare (v. 1). God was also his security: "my rock and my fortress, . . . my shield." It was the Lord who gave him victory, enabling him to subdue other nations (v. 2).

Verses 3-4 sound much like Psalm 8, asking, "What is man . . . or the son of man?" He concluded that man, including the king, "is like a breath, his days are like a passing shadow" (v. 4). Life is transitory. This is one of the themes found often in the Psalter.

The king prayed that God would "bow" the heavens "and come down!" (v. 5). God did precisely that at the birth of Jesus. He prayed that God would come in might, causing volcanoes to erupt and sending a storm whose flashing lightning would be like arrows. At the incarnation God came in a lowly fashion, not as men expected him to come. God often surprises us.

The king prayed for victory over his treaty-breaking enemies (vv. 7-8). He promised to "sing a new song to . . . God," accompanied by "a ten-stringed harp" (v. 9). It is God who gives victories to kings and who rescues and delivers his people (vv. 10-11).

A Prayer for Prosperity (144:12-15)

This wisdom psalm is beautiful. The poet asked that their sons might be vigorous and their daughters stately (v. 12). The people also prayed for bumper crops and fertile flocks (vv. 13-14). They asked for peace and freedom from crisis: "May there be no cry of distress in our streets" (v. 14b).

The concluding line is a triumphant benediction: "Happy the people whose God is the Lord!" (v. 15*b*). This psalm is a prayer for victory in war and prosperity in peacetime. Both are God's undeserved grace to his people.

Psalm 145: "I Will Bless Thy Name Forever"

This acrostic psalm (each verse begins with the succeeding letter of the Hebrew alphabet) features the character of Israel's God and his kingdom. This psalm is readily understood and loved by Christians, as it was by ancient Jews. A profound hymn, the psalm was doubtless used as a solo in Temple worship (v. 1). Its date of composition is thought to be after the Exile.

The Promise to Praise God (145:1-3)

The poet promised that he would praise the Lord "every day" and "for ever." The reason for his praise was the greatness of God. "Great is the Lord, and greatly to be praised" (v. 3).

The Wondrous Works of God (145:4-7)

God is our Creator and our Redeemer. Each generation will remember and proclaim his "mighty acts." Interestingly, the works of God cause us to stand in awe (v. 6) and call forth our praise (v. 7).

The Compassion of God (145:8-9)

"The Lord is gracious and merciful." His anger does not have a short fuse, and his love knows no limits. God is not only merciful to his own people; "The Lord is good to all" (v. 9).

The Kingdom of God (145:10-13)

The kingdom of God means his reign, the area where he rules as Lord. It is made up of individuals who submit to his lordship and is as broad as the church, made up of all born-again believers.

All the faithful ("saints") bless the Lord (v. 10). They declare "the glory of thy kingdom" (v. 11). God's kingdom "endures throughout all generations"—it lasts forever (v. 13). We know this is true because he gives eternal life to all who believe in him. (Note that v. 13 is quoted in Dan. 4:3,34.)

The Faithfulness of God (145:14-21)

God is faithful in both his words and his deeds (v. 13*c*). He lifts up the fallen (v. 14). He provides food for all (v. 15). "Every living thing" receives from the bounty of God's hand (v. 16). The Lord is both just and kind, a wonderful combination (v. 17). He "is near to all who call upon him" (v. 18). To be able to call God "father" means that he is accessible. God hears the cry of those in distress and saves them (v. 19). He preserves those who love him but will destroy the rebellious (v. 20).

The psalm ends as it began, with the promise of praise and an invitation for "all flesh" to "bless his holy name for ever and ever" (v. 21).

Psalm 146: Trust Not Princes, But God

Psalms 146—150 are known as the "hallelujah psalms" because they begin and end with that Hebrew word. Hallelujah is a transliteration of the Hebrew word which literally means "praise the Lord." The social emphasis found in this psalm is much like that of the prophets and of Jesus.

The first two verses are the poet's pledge to "praise the Lord." The word "praise" occurs four times here.

Trust Not in Princes (146:3-4)

The psalmist counseled us not to put our trust in princes for our "help" (literally salvation). They are mere humans, "a son of man" (v. 3). When they die their plans and promises perish with them (v. 4).

Trust in God (146:5-9)

"Happy is he whose help is the God of Jacob" (v. 5). This Beatitude gives us the reason for the poet's praise. His hope is in the Lord who made heaven and earth (v. 6). God "keeps faith forever" (v. 6). His promises never fail since he is eternal.

The Almighty cares about the needs of men:
- He "executes justice for the oppressed."
- He "gives food to the hungry."
- He "sets the prisoners free."
- He "opens the eyes of the blind."
- He "lifts up those who are bowed down."
- He "watches over the sojourners" (strangers and aliens).
- He "upholds the widow and the fatherless."

What an impressive list of social concerns this is. The gospel is one, but its application is both personal and social. God helps those who cannot help themselves.

Concluding Praise (146:10)

God's kingdom and reign will last forever, "to all generations." Hallelujah!

Psalm 147: The Winter Psalm

This hymn praises God for his power and for his providential care. It appears to be three psalms combined into one.

Great Is the Lord Who Builds Up Jerusalem (147:1-6)

God was praised for rebuilding Jerusalem after the Babylonian Exile. God is gracious and worthy of our praise (v. 1). He brought the "outcast" exiles back to Jerusalem, bound up their wounds, and healed them (vv. 2-3). God "lifts up the downtrodden" (v. 6).

Jerusalem was overrun by ruthless invaders and its Temple destroyed three times: Solomon's Temple was plundered and burned in 586 BC; Zerubbabel's in 20 BC; and Herod's in AD 70.

God, who numbered and named the stars, created and controls the universe, keeps us by his providential power despite outward circumstances. "Great is our Lord" (v. 5).

Great Sustainer of Creation (147:7-11)

God is praised for his sustaining providence. "He covers the heavens with clouds," sends rain, makes the grass grow, feeds both birds and beasts (vv. 8-9).

God does not take pleasure in the strength of animals or humans. What pleases him is those who respond to him in faith and hope (vv. 10-11).

Great God of Winter and Spring (147:12-20)

The poet praised the Lord for protecting Jerusalem, blessing her sons, and giving the city peace (v. 13). God also provided them with bread to eat (v. 14).

One almost shivers while reading the psalmist's description of winter. God sends snow and "scatters hoarfrost like ashes" (v. 16). He covers the land with ice—"who can stand before his cold?" (v. 17).

God is also the author of surprising springtime. "He sends forth his word and melts" the ice, snow, and frost. Warm winds blow and refreshing snow waters flow (v. 18).

God has been especially gracious to Israel, giving them his word and his law (vv. 19-20).

The poem is concluded with a hallelujah! It is important that people be sensitive to God's presence in the world and that this sensitivity evoke their praise.

Psalm 148: A Call to Universal Praise

This psalm is a celebration of God as Creator of everything from angels (v. 2) to insects (v. 10). It is actually a series of calls to worship. It has been the inspiration of many Christian hymns, including Francis of Assisi's "All Creatures of Our God and King." Those who trust in the Lord need have no ultimate fear of nature.

Praise in Heaven (148:1-6)

All celestial creatures are called to praise the Lord because he made them and sustains them (see Jer. 31:35-36). Those listed in the psalm include: "All his angels . . . all his host (the heavenly army) . . . sun and moon . . . all you shining stars!" Highest heaven and the waters above the heavens (the source of rain) were invited to praise God. God created them, established them, and controls them (vv. 5-6).

Praise on Earth (148:7-14)

Next, the psalmist summoned all earthly creatures to praise God. He cited the monsters of the sea, "fire and hail, snow and frost, stormy wind"—the forces of nature. God is to be praised by everything from above the heavens to everything beneath the sea! These include "mountains and . . . hills, fruit trees and . . . cedars, beasts and . . . cattle," creeping insects and soaring birds (vv. 9-10).

Kings and common people were called on to praise God. Young men, young women, old people, and children were invited to join "all his saints" (the devout) in praise (vv. 11-12,14).

The Lord's name is to be exalted, and his glory will fill heaven and earth (v. 13). "Praise the Lord!" (v. 14b). God's creation and providence constitute both a call to praise and a summons to service on the part of his people. The praise of God is an obligation as well as a privilege and a joy. It is at the heart of Christian service.

Psalm 149: A Song of Victory

This vigorous psalm of praise is something of a war dance. God's rule can allow no rival, whether enemies or evil or death.

Victory over Enemies (149:1-4)

The people were called on to "sing to the Lord a new song" (v. 1; see Pss. 33:3; 96:1). This was an expression of gratitude to God for a military victory. They praised God with a sacred dance while making melody with the tambourine (timbrel) and harp (lyre).

Divine Judgment on Their Enemies (149:5-9)

The faithful exulted in the glory of their triumph, singing for joy (v. 5). They praised God with their voices and with a sword dance (v. 6). Israel's victory represented vengeance, chastisement, and the execution of judgment on their enemies (vv. 7-9). Their enemies were seen as God's foes, as well.

We find a contrast to this psalm in the teachings of Jesus. He said, "My kingship is not of this world" (John 18:36). Also, Paul taught that our warfare and weapons are not human but spiritual, to be used against evil (see 2 Cor. 10:3-4). Seen in the context of its times, this psalm is understandable. The really sad thing is that we have made so little progress in learning to love our enemies and make them our friends. We still seek vengeance and claim that God is always on our side, despite Jesus' teachings.

Psalm 150: A Doxology of Praise

This festive hymn of praise is a fitting climax to the Psalms—a book of praise to God. It is a doxology which reaches a crescendo of voices and instruments.

Here the psalmist answered four questions: where, why, how, and by whom God is to be praised.

Where Do We Praise God? (150:1)

The Lord is to be praised "in his sanctuary," the Temple in Jerusalem. Also, his glory is to be sung in the world he has created.

Why Do We Praise God? (150:2)

He is due honor "for his mighty deeds" on behalf of his people. He deserves our praise also because of his wonderful character, which is revealed in both nature and in his actions.

How Are We to Praise God? (150:3-5)

Here we have the most extensive list of musical instruments in the Old Testament. God was to be praised "with trumpet sound." Their trumpet was not a horn made of metal but a ram's horn.

The lute and harp or lyre were stringed instruments. A timbrel was a small drum similar to a tambourine. Pipes were probably reed flutes. "Loud clashing cymbals" were also used along with dance in praise of God.

Who Is to Praise God? (150:6)

The poem reached its climax as the poet sang, "Let everything that breathes praise the Lord!" Hallelujah! All creatures including mankind are meant to glorify God, who made and sustains them.

This is a psalm of pure ecstatic praise. Interestingly, the words *breath* and *spirit* are the same word in Hebrew, in Greek, and in Latin. God gives us life (breath) and renews our spirits so that we may praise him. Praise begins and ends with God. Human sin and forgetfulness violate the purpose for which he made us.

The Psalter could not come to a more appropriate close than with Psalm 150. It is a pinnacle of praise in the Old Testament hymnbook of praises. It celebrates God's presence in his world and among his people.